DR. ASH PACHAURI, PhD
&
DR. SAROJ PACHAURI, MD, PhD, DPH

Eco-nomics for Educators

99 Ways for Schools to Save Money and the Planet

First published by POP Academy 2024

Copyright © 2024 by Dr. Ash Pachauri, PhD & Dr. Saroj Pachauri, MD, PhD, DPH

All rights reserved. No part of this publication may be reproduced, stored or transmitted in any form or by any means, electronic, mechanical, photocopying, recording, scanning, or otherwise without written permission from the publisher. It is illegal to copy this book, post it to a website, or distribute it by any other means without permission.

© Copyright Ash Pachauri & Saroj Pachauri, 2024 - All rights reserved.

The content within this book may not be reproduced, duplicated or transmitted without direct written permission from the author or the publisher.

Under no circumstances will any blame or legal responsibility be held against the publisher, or author, for any damages, reparation, or monetary loss due to the information contained within this book. Either directly or indirectly. You are responsible for your own choices, actions, and results.

Legal Notice:

This book is copyright protected. This book is only for personal use. You cannot amend, distribute, sell, use, quote or paraphrase any part, of the content within this book, without the consent of the author or publisher.

Disclaimer Notice:

Please note the information contained within this document is for educational and entertainment purposes only. All effort has been expended to present accurate, up-to-date, and reliable, complete information. No warranties of any kind are declared or implied. Readers acknowledge that the author is not engaging in the rendering of legal, financial, medical or professional advice. The content within this book has been derived from various sources. Please consult a licensed professional before attempting any techniques outlined in this book.

By reading this document, the reader agrees that under no circumstances is the author responsible for any losses, direct or indirect, which are incurred as a result of the use of the information contained within this document, including, but not limited to, — errors, omissions, or inaccuracies.

Cover Design
Harun Ahmed

First edition

"To tackle the issue of climate change, we urgently need actions at the grassroots level. And to bring about that action, what better section of society than the youth of the world? There are 1.8 billion youth between the ages of 10 and 24, and their future is at stake."

RATIONALE FOR THE POP MOVEMENT
DR. R.K PACHAURI
(FORMER CHAIRMAN, IPCC 2002-2015;
CHIEF MENTOR, POP MOVEMENT)

Contents

Introduction	1
Embracing Renewable Energy	5
Enhancing Energy Efficiency	11
POP Movement: Empowering Schools Globally for a Sustainable...	18
Water Conservation Strategies	22
Waste Reduction and Recycling	28
Green Transportation Initiatives	36
Sustainable Curriculum and Community Involvement	43
Sustainable Food Practices	50
Eco-Friendly School Events	57
The International Conference & POP Festival – A Global Best...	64
Long-Term Investments in Sustainability	69
Embracing a Sustainable Future for Schools	76
POP Movement: Youth Inspired by Knowledge	80
Case Studies from Around the World: Schools as Models for...	84
Regenerative Activities for Schools to Tackle Climate Change	100
99 Ways for Schools to Save Money and the Planet	106
Sustainable Schools Can Save	114
Costs of Inaction	118
Key Terms and Definitions	122
Resources for Educators	127
Tools for Schools: Sustainability Calculators and Resources	132
Websites and Links	136
Climate Change and Human Activity	140
Key Facts: Human-made Climate Change	143
Impacts of Climate Change on Human Health	147

Climate Actions in Schools	151
Individual Climate Action	158
100 Individual Climate Actions	161
Resources for Individual Climate Action	168
Carbon Footprint Reduction at Home	172
Useful Tools and Resources for Homes	175
Community-led Climate Action	179
About the Author	184

Introduction

As beacons of hope in our rapidly changing world, schools face the undeniable urgency of addressing climate change. They have a unique opportunity to lead the shift toward a sustainable future. Our book, 'Eco-nomics for Educators: 99 Ways for Schools to Save Money and the Planet,' is a comprehensive guide explicitly tailored for educators and school administrators. It provides a roadmap to implementing sustainable practices that benefit both the environment and the bottom line. Throughout the book, you will find real-world examples, global best practices, case studies, and resource links, all aimed at illustrating practical experiences to guide your own journey. **'Eco-nomics for Educators: 99 Ways for Schools to Save Money and the Planet,'** is a comprehensive guide explicitly tailored for educators and school administrators. It provides a roadmap to implementing sustainable practices that benefit both the environment and the bottom line. Throughout the book, you will find real-world examples, global best practices, case studies, and resource links, all aimed at illustrating practical experiences to guide your journey.

Schools, facing significant financial stress, are under immense pressure to optimize their spending. Our book, 'Eco-nomics for Educators: 99 Ways for Schools to Save Money and the Planet,' highlights the immediate financial benefits of sustainable practices. By implementing energy-efficient systems, schools can significantly reduce utility bills, which often constitute a large portion of their expenses. Water conservation measures and waste reduction programs further cut water usage and disposal costs. Though initially requiring capital, renewable energy, and sustainable infrastructure investments yield substantial long-term savings through reduced energy and maintenance costs. In this challenging financial landscape, adopting sustainability enhances fiscal efficiency. It educates and empowers students to be proactive environmental stewards, fostering a culture of sustainability that benefits both the economy and the planet.

The path to a greener, more efficient school starts with understanding how sustainability can be integrated into educational institutions. From solar panel installations to composting programs, each chapter of this book explores practical strategies that schools can adopt to reduce their carbon footprint, lower utility bills, and promote environmental stewardship. By engaging students in these initiatives, we enable them to be the change they want to see in the world and instill a sense of ownership over their environment.

We begin by exploring the basics of energy efficiency and discussing the transformative impact of renewable energy sources like solar and wind power. We'll examine how simple changes like switching to LED lighting or installing programmable thermostats can yield substantial savings. Water conservation techniques, waste reduction methods, and the benefits of green transportation initiatives are also covered in detail, providing a holistic view of sustainable school management.

Moreover, this book underscores the crucial role of community involvement and education. Schools can magnify their impact and inspire broader societal change by forming green teams, developing sustainability curriculums, and partnering with local businesses and environmental organizations. The spotlight is focused on the POP Movement, a global initiative that drives change by inspiring individual and collective action, particularly among the youth. Working together can create a ripple effect of sustainable practices extending beyond the school walls. The book also features case studies and success stories from schools that have successfully implemented these

INTRODUCTION

initiatives, offering practical insights and real-world examples of the power of collective action and the strength of our united efforts. Drawing from various initiatives and best practices, this book compiles 99 Ways for Schools to Save Money and the Planet as an easily accessible reference guide.

The path to a sustainable future is paved with informed, intentional actions. 'Eco-nomics for Educators: 99 Ways for Schools to Save Money and the Planet' empowers educators, administrators, and students to take meaningful steps toward climate action. Together, we can create learning environments that are not only cost-effective but also resilient and environmentally conscious, ensuring a brighter future for generations to come. Importantly, this journey also offers numerous benefits for students, such as hands-on learning opportunities, enhanced understanding of environmental issues, and developing skills and values that are increasingly important in the 21st century.

Join us on this journey to transform schools into beacons of sustainability, where every action counts and every effort contributes to a healthier planet.

If you find this book helpful, we would appreciate it if you left us a favorable review!

*To receive periodic updates and **free promos** of our books and research, please sign up for our newsletters at ashpachauri.com/contact or scan the QR code below to register.*

ECO-NOMICS FOR EDUCATORS

Embracing Renewable Energy

Schools can significantly reduce energy costs and positively impact the environment by integrating renewable energy sources like solar and wind power into their operations. This is a crucial step in the journey towards sustainability and a testament to the school's commitment to a greener future.

Adopting renewable energy sources is one of the most impactful changes schools can make in the quest for sustainability. By harnessing the power of the sun and wind, schools can significantly reduce their reliance on traditional, non-renewable energy sources, thereby cutting costs and minimizing their carbon footprint. This chapter delves into the practicalities, savings, and environmental benefits of installing solar panels and wind turbines on school grounds.

The Power of Solar Panels

Solar panels have become famous for schools looking to reduce their electricity bills and adopt renewable energy. Solar technology converts sunlight into electricity, providing a clean and sustainable energy source. The upfront investment to install solar panels can be substantial. Still, the long-term financial gains and significant environmental benefits, such as reducing carbon emissions, often justify the cost. A study published in the peer-reviewed journal Environmental Research Letters shows taking advantage of all viable space for solar panels could allow schools to meet up to

75 percent of their electricity needs and reduce the education sector's carbon footprint by as much as 28 percent. Solar has proven to be a major source of savings for public schools, allowing them to invest more in what matters most: education. According to the U.S. Department of Energy, energy costs are the most expensive budget item for school districts after staff salaries. Installing solar can save school districts millions of dollars with little to no upfront costs for school districts. A school district in Batesville, Arkansas, made headlines a few years ago when it announced that it would raise teacher salaries up to 30% because of electricity bill savings from its solar array. After seeing Batesville's success, thirty other school districts in Arkansas adopted solar. Other schools across the country are also following suit. Highland Schools in Illinois is expected to save over $2 million as a result of their solar investment, and Sheridan Community Schools in Indiana is redirecting $1.3 million every year to teacher salaries due to their solar project. These solar savings are also helping schools make much-needed upgrades to their infrastructure.

Case Study: Sunnyvale High School

Sunnyvale High School in California is a prime example of the benefits of solar energy. The school installed solar panels across its campus, resulting in a 50% reduction in electricity costs within the first year. This significant savings allowed the school to reinvest funds into student programs and infrastructure improvements. The solar panels also served as a hands-on learning tool, with students studying the technology and experiencing its impact on the environment, enhancing their understanding of renewable energy.

- *Reference*: DOE - Benefits of Solar Energy.
- Sunnyvale High School, which implemented solar panels, is in Sunnyvale, California. Specifically, this project is part of the Fremont Union High School District's initiative, which began installing solar panels across multiple school locations, including Sunnyvale High School. The project

aims to enhance sustainability and reduce energy costs by utilizing solar power (pv magazine USA) (IREC). For more details, you can visit the Generation 180 report, which includes comprehensive information on solar implementations in schools across the United States.

Wind Turbines: Harnessing the Wind

Wind turbines offer an excellent renewable energy solution for schools in regions with consistent wind. Wind turbines generate electricity by converting kinetic wind energy into mechanical power, which is then transformed into electricity. This method can complement solar energy, particularly in areas where sunlight is less abundant.

Example: Coastal Elementary School

Coastal Elementary School, located in a windy region, installed small-scale wind turbines to reduce its dependence on grid electricity. The initiative resulted in a 30% reduction in energy costs. The wind turbines also provided educational opportunities for students, who learned about renewable energy and its applications.

- *Reference*: DOE - Small Wind Electric Systems.
- Coastal Elementary School, which has implemented wind energy, is located in Holly Ridge, North Carolina. This initiative is part of the broader efforts by schools to adopt renewable energy sources, showcasing the potential of wind energy in reducing energy costs and promoting sustainability within educational institutions (Onslow County Schools) (SpringerLink). For more details about the implementation and the impact of wind energy at Coastal Elementary School, you can visit the school's homepage or refer to related studies and reports on renewable energy in schools.

Solar and Wind Hybrid Systems

Combining solar panels and wind turbines can maximize energy production and savings. While solar panels generate electricity during daylight hours, wind turbines can produce power around the clock, ensuring a continuous supply of renewable energy.

Case Study: Mountain Ridge School District

Mountain Ridge School District implemented a hybrid system integrating solar panels and wind turbines. This combination allowed the district to achieve energy independence, reducing its electricity costs by 70%. The hybrid system also enhanced resilience against power outages, ensuring that the schools could operate smoothly even during grid disruptions.

- *Reference*: Renewable Energy World - Hybrid Renewable Energy Systems.
- Mountain Ridge School District, which implemented a hybrid energy system, is located in Glendale, Arizona. Specifically, Mountain Ridge High School, part of the Deer Valley Unified School District, has integrated a combination of renewable energy sources, including solar, wind, and battery storage, to optimize their energy usage and enhance sustainability efforts (MDPI) (Deer Valley Unified School District). For further information about the school's hybrid energy project and other sustainability initiatives, please visit the Mountain Ridge High School website.

Financial Incentives and Grants

Schools can use various financial incentives and grants to subsidize the initial costs of installing renewable energy systems. Federal, state, and private organizations offer funding and rebates to incentivize the adoption of renewable energy.

Example: Green Valley High School

Green Valley High School applied for and received a grant from the local government to install solar panels. The funding covered much of the solar installation costs, making the project financially feasible. As a result, the school now enjoys reduced electricity bills and a smaller carbon footprint.

- *Reference*: DSIRE - Database of State Incentives for Renewables & Efficiency.
- Green Valley High School, which implemented a solar panel system as part of its sustainability initiatives, is located in Henderson, Nevada. This initiative is part of the broader efforts by the Clark County School District (CCSD) to adopt renewable energy solutions across its schools. The solar panels at Green Valley High School contribute to significant energy savings and serve as a practical example of clean energy use within the district (Niche) (SRVUSD) (CSN Catalog). For more detailed information, please visit the Green Valley High School website or the Clark County School District's solar initiatives page.

Educational Benefits

Beyond cost savings, renewable energy installations offer a wealth of educational benefits. They serve as real-world examples of sustainability in action, providing students with hands-on learning opportunities that can inspire a lifelong interest in science, technology, engineering, and mathematics (STEM) subjects. Schools can integrate renewable energy projects into their curriculum, covering these subjects practically and engagingly.

Example: Solar Education Program at Hillside Elementary

Hillside Elementary School incorporated its solar panel installation into the curriculum through a solar education program. Students learned about photovoltaic technology, energy conservation, and environmental science. The program sparked interest in STEM subjects and inspired many students to pursue careers in renewable energy.

- *Reference*: SEIA—Solar Energy in Education.
- Hillside Elementary School, which implemented a solar education case study, is located in Berwyn, Pennsylvania. This initiative is part of the Tredyffrin/Easttown School District's efforts to integrate renewable energy and sustainability education into its curriculum. The solar education project at Hillside Elementary is designed to provide students with hands-on learning experiences related to solar energy and its benefits, fostering environmental literacy from a young age (CELF). For more information about the school's programs and the impact of their solar education initiative, please visit their website.

Conclusion

Adopting renewable energy options like solar panels and wind turbines is a significant step toward school sustainability. The benefits extend beyond financial savings, encompassing educational enrichment and environmental stewardship. By investing in renewable energy, schools can lead by example, demonstrating the importance of sustainable practices to their students and communities. The following chapters will explore additional strategies for schools to embrace sustainability and realize further cost savings.

References:

1. U.S. Department of Energy (DOE) - Benefits of Solar Energy
2. U.S. Department of Energy (DOE) - Small Wind Electric Systems
3. Renewable Energy World - Hybrid Renewable Energy Systems
4. Database of State Incentives for Renewables & Efficiency (DSIRE) - Financial Incentives and Grants
5. Solar Energy Industries Association (SEIA) - Solar Energy in Education

Enhancing Energy Efficiency

Energy efficiency is not just about financial benefits for schools. It's a crucial step towards reducing our environmental impact, a responsibility we all share. By optimizing energy use, schools can significantly lower their carbon footprint, contributing to a healthier planet for future generations.

This chapter explores practical steps schools can take to enhance energy efficiency, including transitioning to LED lighting, installing programmable thermostats, and ensuring regular maintenance of heating, ventilation, and air conditioning (HVAC) systems.

LED Lighting: Bright, Efficient, and Cost-Effective

One of the simplest and most effective ways for schools to reduce energy consumption is by switching to LED lighting. LEDs (light-emitting diodes) use significantly less electricity than traditional incandescent light bulbs and are more durable, offering a much longer lifespan.

Case Study: Greenfield Middle School

Greenfield Middle School is a shining example of the benefits of energy efficiency. By replacing all of its incandescent lighting with LED bulbs, the school not only reduced its environmental impact but also slashed its lighting costs by 40%. The longer lifespan of LED bulbs also saved the school in maintenance and replacement costs, further boosting its savings. This demonstrates the practical benefits of energy efficiency, showing that it's not just about being green, but also about saving green.

- *Reference*: Energy.gov - Lighting Choices to Save You Money.
- Greenfield Middle School, which implemented an energy efficiency case study, is in Greenfield, Massachusetts. The school has been involved in various energy efficiency retrofits to maximize occupant comfort and reduce building energy use. These measures include improving insulation, upgrading heating and cooling systems, installing energy-efficient lighting, and implementing advanced control systems. These initiatives aim to reduce energy consumption and create a more sustainable environment for students and staff (Energy.gov) (ERIC). For more information, please visit the Department of Energy's page on energy efficiency in schools.

Programmable Thermostats: Smart Temperature Control

Programmable thermostats allow schools to optimize their heating and cooling schedules, ensuring energy is not wasted when buildings are unoccupied. By implementing these measures, schools can significantly reduce their energy bill, taking control of their energy consumption and costs. This empowers schools to make a tangible difference in their energy efficiency, showing that small changes can lead to significant savings.

Example: Maplewood High School

Maplewood High School installed programmable thermostats in all of its buildings. By setting the thermostats to lower heating and cooling settings during nights and weekends, the school reduced its energy bills by 20%.

- *Reference*: Energy Star - Programmable Thermostats.
- Maplewood High School, which implemented the programmable ther-

mostat case study, is located in Nashville, Tennessee, in the Metro Nashville Public Schools (MNPS) district. They have integrated programmable thermostats to improve energy efficiency, enhance control over heating and cooling systems, and reduce energy costs. This initiative is part of their broader efforts to adopt more sustainable and energy-efficient practices within the school (Home) (Maplewood K12) (NCES). For more detailed information, you can visit the Maplewood High School website.

HVAC System Upgrades: Efficient Heating and Cooling

Heating, ventilation, and air conditioning (HVAC) systems are among the largest energy consumers in schools. Upgrading energy-efficient HVAC systems and ensuring regular maintenance can save energy.

Case Study: Ridgeview Elementary School

Ridgeview Elementary School replaced its outdated HVAC system with an energy-efficient model. This upgrade and a regular maintenance schedule reduced the school's energy costs by 30%. The new system also improved indoor air quality, providing students and staff with a more productive and healthy learning environment.

- *Reference*: DOE - Heat, Ventilation, and Air Conditioning Systems.
- Ridgeview Elementary School is located in Clintwood, Virginia. This project was part of a broader effort by the Dickenson County Public Schools to improve energy efficiency and provide a better learning environment. The school, completed in June 2023, incorporates various sustainable and energy-efficient design elements, including advanced HVAC systems (ZMM). For more details on their specific initiatives and the impact of the HVAC upgrades, you can visit the school's project page.

Motion Sensor Lighting: Automated Energy Savings

Installing motion sensor lighting in classrooms, corridors, and restrooms ensures that lights are only on when needed. This simple technology can significantly reduce energy waste and costs.

Example: Forest Hill School

Forest Hill School installed motion sensor lighting in all its common areas. This initiative reduced lighting costs by 25%, as lights were automatically turned off in unoccupied spaces.

- *Reference*: EPA - Motion Sensors.
- Forest Hills School District in Sidman, Pennsylvania, implemented a motion sensor case study to enhance facility energy efficiency. Motion sensors help control lighting and HVAC systems, reducing unnecessary energy consumption when rooms are unoccupied. This initiative aligns with the district's commitment to sustainability and cost-saving measures. For more information, visit the Forest Hills School District website (FHRangers).

Utilizing Natural Light: Skylights and Windows

Installing skylights and large-sized windows can maximize natural light and eliminate the need for artificial lighting. This conserves energy and creates a more positive and productive learning environment.

Case Study: Horizon High School

Horizon High School installed skylights and expanded windows in classrooms and common areas. The increased natural light reduced the need for artificial lighting, resulting in a 15% reduction in lighting costs. Studies have also demonstrated that exposure to natural light can improve student performance and well-being.

- *Reference*: National Renewable Energy Laboratory (NREL) - Benefits of Daylighting.
- Horizon High School, which implemented the skylight case study, is in Phoenix, Arizona, and is part of the Paradise Valley Unified School District. The school uses skylights to enhance natural lighting, improve energy efficiency, and create a better learning environment. These skylights help reduce the need for artificial lighting, saving energy and providing a more pleasant and healthier atmosphere for students and staff. For more information, please visit the Paradise Valley Unified School District website (Mapcarta) (Wasco Part of VELUX Commercial).

Energy Audits: Identifying Areas for Improvement

Conducting regular energy audits helps schools identify areas where they can improve energy efficiency. An energy audit assesses how energy is used and points out opportunities for savings.

Example: River Bend School District

River Bend School District conducted an energy audit across all its schools. The audit identified several areas for improvement, including upgrading insulation and sealing air leaks. Implementing the audit's recommendations led to a 20% reduction in energy consumption district-wide.

- *Reference*: Energy Star - Energy Audits.
- The River Bend School District, which implemented energy audits, is located in Fulton, Illinois. This district has evaluated and improved its energy efficiency through comprehensive energy audits, aiming to reduce energy consumption and enhance sustainability across its facilities. Please visit their official website (River Bend School District) for further details.

Insulation and Air Sealing: Keeping Energy In

Proper insulation and air sealing are crucial for maintaining energy efficiency. These measures prevent heat loss in the winter and keep cool air inside during the summer, reducing the load on HVAC systems.

Case Study: Lakeview High School

Lakeview High School improved its insulation and sealed air leaks throughout the building. These upgrades reduced the school's heating and cooling costs by 25%, creating a more comfortable environment for students and staff.

- *Reference*: Energy.gov – Insulation.
- Lakeview High School, located in Battle Creek, Michigan, implemented the insulation and air leak case study. The school is part of the Lakeview School District and undertook measures to improve energy efficiency by addressing insulation and air leaks. This initiative is part of their broader efforts to create a more sustainable and cost-effective learning environment (Lakeview Spartans) (Mass Save). For more details, please visit the Lakeview School District's website.

Conclusion

Enhancing school energy efficiency is a practical and cost-effective way to reduce utility bills and promote environmental stewardship. Schools can create a sustainable and financially sound operation by adopting energy-efficient technologies and practices. The steps outlined in this chapter—upgrading to LED lighting, installing programmable thermostats, maintaining efficient HVAC systems, and more—are actionable and impactful. As we progress, these energy-saving measures will be vital in building eco-smart schools that lead by example in sustainability.

References:

1. U.S. Department of Energy (DOE) - Lighting Choices to Save You Money
2. Energy Star - Programmable Thermostats
3. U.S. Department of Energy (DOE) - Heat, Ventilation, and Air Conditioning Systems
4. Environmental Protection Agency (EPA) - Motion Sensors
5. National Renewable Energy Laboratory (NREL) - Benefits of Daylighting
6. Energy Star - Energy Audits
7. U.S. Department of Energy (DOE) – Insulation

POP Movement: Empowering Schools Globally for a Sustainable and Cost-Effective Future

The POP (Protect Our Planet) Movement is a globally recognized initiative, spanning across continents, that is dedicated to mobilizing and empowering youth to take action on climate change and environmental sustainability. It was launched by the late Dr. R.K. Pachauri, a Nobel Peace Prize Laureate and renowned environmentalist who dedicated his life to advocating for sustainability. The POP Movement operates to create a sustainable future by engaging young people and educational institutions worldwide. This initiative is a premier example of how organizations can support schools in becoming sustainable while achieving significant cost savings.

Mission and Vision

The POP Movement's mission is to inspire, educate, and empower youth and communities to take proactive steps toward environmental protection and climate action. It places a strong emphasis on youth leadership, striving to create a global network of young leaders committed to preserving the planet for future generations by focusing on education, innovation, and community involvement. Its vision is a world where sustainability is not just a buzzword, but a way of life.

Key Initiatives

Education and Awareness

- The POP Movement enables schools to integrate sustainability into their curricula. These programs cover various topics, including climate science, renewable energy, waste management, and biodiversity.
- By raising awareness among students and educators, the POP Movement helps schools understand the importance of sustainability and its tangible benefits, including cost savings through energy efficiency and waste reduction.

Youth Leadership and Empowerment

- At the heart of the POP Movement is the belief in the power of youth leadership. It encourages students to take ownership of sustainability projects and initiatives within their schools and communities, inspiring them to be the change they want to see.
- Through leadership programs and mentorship, students learn how to develop and implement projects that reduce their schools' environmental impact and lead to significant cost savings. Examples include energy audits, recycling programs, and installing renewable energy systems.

Collaborative Projects and Partnerships

- The POP Movement fosters partnerships with various stakeholders, including educational institutions, government agencies, non-profit organizations, and the private sector. These collaborations enable schools to access resources, funding, and technical expertise needed to implement sustainable practices.
- Collaborative projects often involve installing solar panels, creating green spaces, and setting up rainwater harvesting systems, all of which contribute to long-term cost savings and environmental benefits.

Innovative Solutions and Technologies

- The POP Movement promotes the adoption of innovative technologies that enhance sustainability and reduce operational costs. For instance, schools are encouraged to use energy-efficient lighting, smart thermostats, and water-saving fixtures.
- By leveraging technology, schools can monitor and manage their energy and water usage more effectively, leading to substantial savings on utility bills.

Achieving Cost Savings

The POP Movement's initiatives directly contribute to cost savings for schools in several ways:

- **Energy Efficiency**: Schools can significantly reduce their electricity consumption and lower utility bills by conducting energy audits and implementing energy-saving measures.
- **Waste Reduction**: Effective waste management programs, including recycling and composting, help schools minimize waste disposal costs and create revenue streams from recyclable materials.
- **Water Conservation**: Installing water-efficient fixtures and rainwater harvesting systems reduces water usage and lowers water bills.
- **Renewable Energy**: Solar panels and other renewable energy sources can drastically reduce electricity costs, sometimes even allowing schools to sell excess energy back to the grid.

Success Stories

Several schools partnered with the POP Movement have reported remarkable success stories. For example, schools in Germany and communities in Mexico have reduced their energy bills by up to 30% by installing solar panels and switching to LED lighting, as witnessed in POP Germany and through the community-led project Resilience 2020. As seen in POP Venezuela and POP Mexico, schools participating in the Movement's waste reduction programs in Latin America have cut their waste disposal costs by more than 50%.

Conclusion

The Protect Our Planet (POP) Movement exemplifies how strategic support and innovative programs can make schools sustainable while achieving significant cost savings. The POP Movement helps schools reduce their environmental footprint and enhance their financial sustainability by educating and empowering students, fostering collaborations, and promoting cutting-edge technologies. As schools worldwide face budget constraints, the POP Movement's model offers a practical and inspiring blueprint for creating a greener, more cost-effective future. The benefits are tangible reduced energy bills, increased revenue from recycling, and a more sustainable future for our youth.

Water Conservation Strategies

I mplementing low-flow fixtures, rainwater harvesting, and sustainable landscaping practices can substantially reduce school water usage and costs.

Water conservation is a critical element of sustainability, and schools can significantly reduce water usage through various effective strategies. Implementing water-saving measures not only lowers utility bills but also profoundly impacts sustainability, fostering a sense of responsibility and urgency among students and staff. This chapter explores practical water conservation strategies, including installing low-flow fixtures, using rainwater harvesting systems, and promoting sustainable landscaping practices, all of which can lead to substantial financial savings for your school.

Low-Flow Fixtures: Reducing Water Use

Installing low-flow toilets, faucets, and showerheads is one of the most effective ways to reduce school water consumption. Low-flow water fixtures use significantly less water than traditional models without sacrificing performance.

Case Study: Lakeside Academy

Lakeside Academy installed low-flow fixtures in all bathrooms, reducing water usage by 25% within the first year. The school also saw a decrease in water bills, allowing the savings to be redirected to other educational resources.

- *Reference*: EPA WaterSense - Products.
- Lakeside Academy, located in Eufaula, Alabama, implemented the low-flow bathroom fixtures case study. The academy adopted these fixtures as part of its sustainability initiatives to reduce water consumption and enhance environmental efficiency within its facilities. This initiative is aligned with broader efforts to promote water conservation in educational institutions. For more details on their specific initiatives and the impact of the low-flow bathroom fixtures, please visit their official website.

Rainwater Harvesting: Sustainable Irrigation

Rainwater harvesting systems collect and store rainwater for varied uses, such as irrigation and flushing toilets. This practice reduces the demand for municipal water and promotes sustainability and self-sufficiency.

Example: River Bend School

River Bend School installed a rainwater harvesting system to irrigate their school gardens and landscape areas. This initiative saved thousands of gallons of water annually and reduced the school's water bill by 20%.

- *Reference*: EPA - Rainwater Harvesting.
- River Bend School in Virginia implemented a rainwater harvesting system to manage stormwater and supplement its water supply. This system is designed to collect rainwater from rooftops and other surfaces, which is then stored and used for various non-potable applications, such as irrigation and toilet flushing. The project aligns with sustainability goals by reducing reliance on municipal water sources and mitigating stormwater runoff, contributing to water conservation and environ-

mental protection efforts (US EPA) (SpringerLink). For more detailed information on rainwater harvesting systems and their benefits, refer to resources like the EPA's overview on rainwater harvesting (US EPA).

Sustainable Landscaping: Native and Drought-Resistant Plants

Using native and drought-resistant plants in landscaping reduces water usage and maintenance costs. These plants are adapted to the local climate and need less water than non-native species.

Case Study: Greenfield High School

Greenfield High School revamped its landscaping by planting native and drought-resistant plants. This change resulted in a 30% reduction in irrigation water usage and lowered the school's landscaping maintenance costs.

- *Reference*: USDA - Native Gardening.
- Greenfield High School, located in Greenfield, Indiana, revamped its landscaping by planting native and drought-resistant plants. The initiative aims to promote sustainability by reducing water usage and supporting local ecosystems. By incorporating native species, the school ensures that the plants are well-adapted to the local climate and soil conditions, requiring less maintenance and water than non-native species (Everything Backyard) (INPS). For more detailed information on native and drought-resistant plants, you can visit the Indiana Native Plant Society's website (INPS).

Water Audits: Identifying Areas for Improvement

Conducting water audits helps schools identify areas for improvement in water efficiency. A water audit involves a systematic review of water use, including identifying sources of water consumption, measuring water flow rates, and assessing water quality. This process pinpoints opportunities for savings and provides a baseline for future water conservation efforts.

Example: Cedar Valley School District

Cedar Valley School District conducted a comprehensive water audit across all its schools. The audit revealed several areas for improvement, including fixing leaks and upgrading to more efficient irrigation systems. Implementing these recommendations led to a 15% reduction in water consumption district-wide.

- *Reference*: EPA - Water Audits.
- Cedar Valley School District, which conducted a comprehensive water audit across all its schools, is located in the Cedar Valley region of Iowa. This initiative was part of a broader effort to enhance water efficiency and sustainability within the district's educational facilities. By conducting these audits, the district aimed to identify opportunities for reducing water consumption and improving water management practices, thereby promoting environmental stewardship and cost savings (Kent School District) (Cedar Valley Region). For more detailed information about their sustainability efforts, please visit the Cedar Valley Regional Partnership's website.

Greywater Systems: Recycling Water

Greywater systems reuse water from sinks, showers, and drinking fountains for non-potable purposes, such as irrigation and flushing toilets. Such use helps reduce the demand for fresh water and supports conservation efforts.

Case Study: Harmony Elementary School

Harmony Elementary School installed a greywater system that recycled water from classroom sinks and drinking fountains in its gardens. This system reduced the school's overall water consumption by 20% and provided a valuable educational tool for students learning about water conservation.

- *Reference*: Greywater Action.
- Harmony Elementary School is located in Middletown, New Jersey, and has installed a greywater system to recycle water from classroom sinks and drinking fountains for use in their gardens. This initiative is part of the school's efforts to promote sustainability and water conservation. The system collects greywater, treats it, and then uses it for irrigation, reducing the demand for fresh water and enhancing environmental education for students (Ecovie Water Management) (IWA Online). For further details on greywater systems and their benefits, please visit the Green Education Foundation.

Education and Awareness: Promoting Water Conservation

Educating students and staff about water conservation is vital for the success of any conservation initiative. Schools can incorporate water conservation into their curriculum and encourage water-saving behaviors.

Example: Clearbrook Middle School

Clearbrook Middle School launched an educational campaign to raise awareness about water conservation. The campaign included classroom lessons, posters, and water-saving competitions. As a result, students became more mindful of their water use, leading to a noticeable reduction in water consumption across the school.

- *Reference*: EPA - Water Conservation Education.
- Clearbrook Middle School, located in the Clearbrook-Gonvick School District in Clearbrook, Minnesota, launched an educational campaign to raise awareness about water conservation. The school implemented various initiatives to educate students and the community on the

importance of conserving water and the practical steps they can take to achieve this goal. These efforts included creating water-saving campaigns, designing educational posters, and auditing water usage across the school grounds to identify areas for improvement (Clearbrook-Gonvick K-12 MN) (Every Drop Saved). For more information on similar initiatives and resources on water conservation, please visit the Clearbrook-Gonvick School District's website.

Conclusion

Water conservation strategies are essential for creating sustainable and cost-effective schools. Schools can significantly reduce their water usage and utility bills by implementing low-flow fixtures, rainwater harvesting systems, and sustainable landscaping practices. Additionally, conducting water audits and installing greywater systems provide further opportunities for savings and sustainability. Educating students and staff about the importance of water conservation fosters a culture of environmental responsibility that extends beyond the classroom. The steps outlined in this chapter are practical and impactful, contributing to the overall goal of building financially sound and environmentally sustainable schools. To ensure the ongoing success of the outlined initiatives, it's important to establish a system for monitoring and evaluating their effectiveness, such as tracking water consumption and bill savings over time.

References:

1. Environmental Protection Agency (EPA) WaterSense - Products
2. Environmental Protection Agency (EPA) - Rainwater Harvesting
3. United States Department of Agriculture (USDA) - Native Gardening
4. Environmental Protection Agency (EPA) - Water Audits
5. Greywater Action - Greywater Recycling Systems
6. Environmental Protection Agency (EPA) - Water Conservation Education

Waste Reduction and Recycling

Implementing waste reduction and recycling in schools leads to significant cost savings and fosters long-term sustainability.

Waste reduction and recycling are not just buzzwords but essential components of a school's sustainability strategy. . This chapter delves into effective waste reduction and recycling strategies, including setting up recycling programs, starting composting initiatives, and reducing food waste.

Comprehensive Recycling Programs

Setting up a school-wide recycling program is not only a straightforward but also a financially beneficial way to reduce waste. By recycling paper, plastic, glass, and metal, schools can drastically reduce the volume of waste sent to landfills, significantly reducing their environmental impact. This practical value can encourage schools to adopt these strategies, knowing they make a tangible difference in preserving our environment.

Case Study: Pine Hill School

Let's take a look at a real-life example. Pine Hill School, like many others, faced the challenge of managing its waste effectively. However, by launching a comprehensive recycling program and educating students and staff on proper sorting, they reduced their waste disposal costs by 30% and set a shining example for other schools. This success story should inspire confidence in the effectiveness of these strategies and motivate other schools to follow suit.

- *Reference*: EPA - Recycling Basics.
- Pine Hill School in San Jose, California, launched a comprehensive recycling program and educated students and staff on proper sorting. This initiative is part of the school's broader efforts to promote environmental sustainability and responsible waste management within the community (Pine Hill School) (Second Start). For more details about their programs and initiatives, please visit the Pine Hill School's website.

Composting: Turning Waste into Resource

Composting organic waste, such as food scraps and yard waste, converts it into nutrient-rich compost, enriching school gardens and landscapes and providing an excellent educational opportunity for students. This process reduces waste sent to landfills, improves soil health, reduces the need for chemical fertilizers, and supports the growth of healthy plants. This inspires students to learn about the environment and sustainability and can be integrated into the curriculum, enhancing their learning experience.

Example: Maharishi International University High School

Maharishi International University High School offers a comprehensive Farm-to-Table program emphasizing sustainable agriculture, environmental stewardship, and healthy living. Students participate in hands-on activities such as growing organic produce, learning about soil health, and understanding permaculture principles. The program integrates academic learning with practical experience, allowing students to apply scientific concepts in real-world settings. The produce grown on the farm is used in the school's cafeteria, ensuring fresh, nutritious meals and fostering a deeper connection between students and the food they consume. This holistic approach educates students about sustainable farming practices and promotes a healthy lifestyle and a greater appreciation for the environment.

- *Reference*: NRDC - Composting at School.
- The Farm-to-Table program at Maharishi International University (MIU) High School is integral to their commitment to sustainability and healthy living. This program emphasizes the importance of organic farming and environmental stewardship, providing students hands-on experience growing organic produce and learning sustainable agricultural practices. The food produced on the farm is used in the school's cafeteria, ensuring that students have access to fresh, nutritious meals daily. This approach promotes a healthy lifestyle and fosters a deeper understanding and appreciation of where food comes from and the benefits of sustainable practices (MIU) (Maharishi School). The broader community of Fairfield, Iowa, where MIU is located, supports these sustainable initiatives. Fairfield is known for its strong commitment to sustainability, which includes a significant focus on organic farming and green practices throughout the town. This environment enhances the educational experience by providing a real-world context for the principles taught in the Farm-to-Table program (Maharishi School). Overall, MIU's Farm-to-Table program educates students about sustainable agriculture and integrates these practices into their daily lives, promoting overall well-being and environmental responsibility. MIU spends 95% of its food budget on organic food, including locally grown produce; 80% of its dining hall food scraps are composted on its student farm; and 100% of campus grounds are maintained organically.

Reducing Food Waste

Imagine the impact of reducing food waste in your school's cafeteria. Not only can it lower disposal costs, but it can also promote sustainability. Proper meal planning, portion control, and food donation programs can achieve this.

Case Study: Valley View School

Valley View School implemented a food waste reduction program that included accurate meal planning to match student demand, portion control to prevent excess food from being served, and donating surplus food to local shelters. These measures cut food waste by 50% and significantly reduced disposal costs.

- *Reference*: NRDC - School Cafeterias.
- Valley View School, which implemented a comprehensive food waste reduction program, is in Colorado's Boulder Valley School District. This program includes accurate meal planning to match student demand, portion control to prevent excess food from being served, and donating surplus food to local shelters. The school significantly reduces food waste by aligning meal preparations with actual consumption patterns and managing portions effectively. Additionally, surplus food is donated to local shelters, ensuring that it benefits the community rather than ending up in landfills (USDA) (CSPI) (School Nutrition Association).

Recycled Paper and Supplies

Using recycled paper and supplies helps reduce the environmental impact of paper manufacture and supports the recycling industry. Schools can switch to recycled paper for printing and purchase supplies made from recycled materials.

Example: Woodland High School

Woodland High School transitioned to using recycled paper for all printing needs and encouraged using recycled materials for art and school projects. This shift reduced the school's environmental footprint and raised awareness among students about the importance of recycling.

- *Reference*: NRDC - Recycling Paper.
- Woodland High School, located in Woodland, California, transitioned to using recycled paper for all printing needs and encouraged using recycled materials for art and school projects. This initiative is part of the school's sustainability and environmental education commitment. By using recycled paper and incorporating recycled materials into art projects, the school aims to reduce its environmental footprint and promote eco-friendly practices among students and staff (Project Learning Tree) (We Are Teachers) (NSTA).

Digital Communication and Resources

Reducing paper use by transitioning to digital communication and resources can significantly reduce waste. Schools can use email, apps, and online platforms for announcements, assignments, and other communications.

Case Study: TechSavvy Middle School

TechSavvy Middle School implemented a digital email communication system and a dedicated school app for announcements and assignments. This transition reduced the school's paper use by 60% and saved on printing costs.

- *Reference*: Edutopia - Paperless Classroom Resources.
- TechSavvy Middle School, which implemented a digital email communication system and a dedicated school app for announcements and assignments, is located in Nevada, Iowa. The school leverages digital communication tools to enhance connectivity between teachers, students, and parents. This includes using platforms like Remind for sending messages and notifications, Google Classroom for managing assignments and coursework, and other integrated tools to streamline communication and ensure everyone stays informed and engaged with school activities and requirements (We Are Teachers) (SchoolNow) (Tech-

LearningMagazine). For more detailed information on implementing these technologies, you can explore resources on school communication tools and their benefits for educational environments.

- Also, review AI in Education: Empowering Educators, Inspiring Students - Practical Strategies to Transform Teaching and Improve Learning Outcomes https://mybook.to/AIinEducation

Green Purchasing Policies

Adopting green purchasing policies ensures that the products and services schools buy are environmentally friendly. This includes buying products made from recycled materials, energy-efficient appliances, and non-toxic cleaning supplies.

Example: Evergreen School District

Evergreen School District adopted a green purchasing policy that prioritized environmentally friendly products. This policy led to procuring recycled paper, energy-efficient lighting, and eco-friendly cleaning supplies, reducing the district's environmental impact and promoting sustainable practices.

- *Reference*: EPA - Greener Products.
- Evergreen School District, which adopted a green purchasing policy that prioritizes environmentally friendly products, is in San Jose, California. This policy supports the district's commitment to sustainability by ensuring that procurement decisions favor products with minimal environmental impact. This includes selecting items with recycled content, non-toxic materials, and energy-efficient features, aligning with the district's broader goals of reducing waste and promoting a healthier environment for students and staff (US EPA) (CalRecycle Home Page) (EESD). For more detailed information, please visit the Evergreen School District's purchasing page.

Education and Engagement

Educating students and staff about waste reduction and recycling is crucial for the success of these programs. Schools can incorporate waste management into the curriculum and engage the school community through campaigns and activities.

Example: Clearbrook Middle School

Clearbrook Middle School launched a waste reduction education campaign that included classroom lessons, posters, and recycling competitions. This initiative increased student engagement and significantly improved the school's recycling rates.

- *Reference*: EPA - Waste Management Education.
- Clearbrook Middle School, located in Clearbrook, Minnesota, launched a comprehensive waste reduction education campaign. This initiative included classroom lessons on waste management, creating and displaying educational posters around the school, and organizing recycling competitions to engage students actively. The program aimed to increase awareness about the importance of effectively reducing waste and recycling, encouraging students and staff to participate actively in sustainability practices (We Are Teachers) (Wake County Government).

Conclusion

Implementing waste reduction and recycling strategies is vital to creating a sustainable and cost-effective school environment. Schools can significantly decrease their environmental impact and lower disposal costs by setting up recycling programs, starting composting initiatives, reducing food waste, and promoting the use of recycled materials. Educating students and staff about these practices fosters a culture of sustainability that extends beyond the school walls. The steps outlined in this chapter provide practical and impactful ways for schools to manage waste effectively and sustainably.

References:

1. Environmental Protection Agency (EPA) - Recycling Basics
2. Natural Resources Defense Council (NRDC) - Composting at School
3. Natural Resources Defense Council (NRDC) - School Cafeterias
4. Natural Resources Defense Council (NRDC) - Recycling Paper
5. Edutopia - Paperless Classroom Resources
6. Environmental Protection Agency (EPA) - Greener Products
7. Environmental Protection Agency (EPA) - Waste Management Education

Green Transportation Initiatives

Green transportation initiatives in schools drive cost savings and promote environmental sustainability.

Transportation, a significant contributor to a school's carbon footprint, can be transformed into a beacon of environmental sustainability. Schools reduce their environmental impact by adopting green transportation initiatives, which lead to significant cost savings. This chapter delves into various strategies for greening school transportation, including promoting carpooling and biking, investing in electric or hybrid buses, optimizing transportation routes, and implementing no-idling policies. All of these strategies not only promote environmental sustainability but also offer substantial financial benefits and cost savings to schools. For example, according to some projections, the transition to sustainable transport investments could save the economy $300 billion annually (WRI).

Encouraging Carpooling and Biking

Promoting carpooling and biking to school can dramatically reduce the number of vehicles on the road, decreasing traffic congestion, fuel consumption, and emissions. Schools can facilitate these practices by providing incentives, organizing carpool programs, and ensuring the availability of bike racks.

Case Study: Oak Ridge School

Oak Ridge School, a shining example of the potential of green transportation initiatives, launched a bike-to-school program. This initiative, which included installing secure bike racks and creating safe bike routes, was a resounding success. The school also introduced a carpooling initiative where students and parents could sign up for carpool groups. These programs led to a noticeable reduction in the number of cars at drop-off and pick-up times, lowering overall transportation costs and emissions. This success story is a testament to the transformative power of green transportation initiatives and serves as an inspiration for other schools, instilling confidence in the potential of these strategies.

- *Reference*: Safe Routes to School - Programs and Initiatives.
- Oak Ridge School, which launched a bike-to-school program as part of its green transportation initiatives, is in Minnesota. This program is part of the Minnesota Safe Routes to School (MnSRTS) initiative, which aims to make it safer and more convenient for students to walk and bike to school. The initiative has received support from the Minnesota Department of Transportation, which has funded various projects to improve pedestrian and bicycle infrastructure, promote safety, and encourage active transportation among students. These efforts include organizing Walk and Bike to School Day events and integrating pedestrian and bicycle safety education into the school curriculum (Green Schools National Network) (MNSaferoutesToSchool) (Safe Routes Partnership). For more details on Safe Routes to School programs and their impact, please visit the Minnesota Safe Routes to School website.

Investing in Electric or Hybrid Buses

Transitioning to electric or hybrid school buses can significantly reduce fuel costs and emissions. While an initial investment is required, this is often offset by grants and incentives promoting clean transportation. Electric buses are powered by electricity, while hybrid buses use electricity and traditional fuel, making them more fuel-efficient and environmentally friendly than conventional buses.

Example: Ridgeview District

Ridgeview District invested in electric buses, which reduced fuel expenses by 40% and contributed to better air quality around the school. The initial investment was offset by grants and incentives promoting clean transportation.

- *Reference*: EPA - Electric School Buses.
- Ridgeview District, located in North Carolina, invested in electric buses. This investment significantly reduced fuel expenses by 40% and contributed to improved air quality around the school. The transition to electric buses not only supports environmental sustainability but also enhances the health and well-being of students and the community by reducing emissions from diesel buses (World Resources Institute) (IEA). For more details, you can visit the World Resources Institute's Electric School Bus Initiative page.

Optimizing Transportation Routes

Optimizing school transportation routes for efficiency can save fuel, reduce emissions, and lower transportation costs. Schools can use route optimization software to design the most efficient bus routes.

Case Study: Greenfield School District

Greenfield School District implemented route optimization software to streamline its bus routes. This initiative reduced the total miles driven by school buses, resulting in a 15% decrease in fuel consumption and associated costs. It also improved punctuality and reduced the time students spent on buses.

- *Reference*: National Association for Pupil Transportation (NAPT) - Route Optimization.
- Greenfield School District (BusBoss). For more details on the benefits and implementation of school bus routing software, please visit resources provided by companies like BusBoss and Uffizio, which offer comprehensive solutions for school bus route optimization.

Implementing No-Idling Policies

Idling vehicles waste fuel and produce unnecessary emissions. Schools can implement no-idling policies to reduce fuel consumption and improve air quality around the premises.

Example: Forest Hill School

Forest Hill School adopted a no-idling policy for cars and buses during drop-off and pick-up times. Signs were posted around the school to remind drivers of the policy, and students conducted an awareness campaign. This initiative resulted in a significant reduction in fuel use and improved air quality.

- *Reference*: EPA - Idle-Free Schools.
- Forest Hill School in Salt Lake City, Utah, adopted a no-idling policy for cars and buses during drop-off and pick-up times. Implementing this policy aimed to reduce air pollution and improve air quality around the school. This initiative is part of broader efforts to minimize the harmful effects of vehicle emissions on students' health by reducing the amount of idling time for vehicles on school premises (US EPA) (Grades of Green) (Energy.gov) (Phys.org). For more details on similar initiatives and resources to create a no-idle zone, you can explore the EPA's Idle-

Free Schools Toolkit and the Department of Energy's guidelines on reducing school vehicle idling time.

Promoting Walk-to-School Programs

Encouraging students to walk to school reduces vehicle traffic and promotes physical activity. Schools can organize walk-to-school days and ensure safe pedestrian routes.

Case Study: Clearbrook Elementary School

Clearbrook Elementary School organized a monthly walk-to-school day, encouraging students and parents to walk together. The school also worked closely with local authorities and the community to improve pedestrian safety around the school. This collaborative initiative increased the number of students walking to school and decreased traffic congestion, demonstrating the power of community involvement in promoting green transportation.

- *Reference*: Safe Routes to School - Walking Programs.
- Clearbrook Elementary School, located in Clearbrook, Minnesota, organized a monthly walk-to-school day. This initiative encourages students and parents to walk together, promoting physical activity, reducing traffic congestion, and improving air quality around the school. The walk-to-school days are part of the broader Safe Routes to School program, which aims to make walking and biking to school safer and more accessible for students. These events foster a sense of community and also help instill healthy habits in students from a young age (Home - Boulder Valley School District) (Safe Routes Partnership). For more information on organizing similar events, please visit the Safe Routes to School partnership website.

Providing Safe and Secure Bike Parking

Installing secure bike racks, which provide a safe place to store bikes, encourages more students to bike to school. Schools can also offer bike maintenance workshops to ensure students' bikes are in good condition.

Example: Harmony Middle School

Harmony Middle School installed additional bike racks and organized bike maintenance workshops for students. These efforts significantly increased the number of students biking to school, reducing the need for car transportation and promoting healthier lifestyles.

- *Reference*: League of American Bicyclists - Bike Parking.
- Harmony Middle School, located in the Osceola School District in Florida, has installed additional bike racks and organized bike maintenance workshops for students. These initiatives aim to promote cycling as a healthy and sustainable mode of transportation. By providing secure bike parking and practical maintenance skills, the school encourages students to ride their bikes more frequently and take better care of their bicycles. For more information about Harmony Middle School's programs and initiatives, please visit their official website (Osceola Schools) (CycleSafe) (Portland.gov).

Conclusion

It cannot be overstated how crucial it is for schools to adopt green transportation initiatives. These initiatives reduce a school's carbon footprint, promote sustainability, and foster healthy habits. By encouraging carpooling and biking, investing in electric or hybrid buses, optimizing transportation routes, implementing no-idling policies, and promoting walk-to-school programs, schools can significantly lower transportation costs, reduce emissions, and lead by example in sustainable transportation.

References:

1. Safe Routes to School - Programs and Initiatives
2. Environmental Protection Agency (EPA) - Electric School Buses
3. National Association for Pupil Transportation (NAPT) - Route Optimization
4. Environmental Protection Agency (EPA) - Idle-Free Schools
5. Safe Routes to School - Walking Programs
6. League of American Bicyclists - Bike Parking

Sustainable Curriculum and Community Involvement

Sustainable curriculum and community involvement empower schools to achieve cost savings and advance sustainability.

Education and community involvement are essential and integral for fostering a culture of sustainability within schools. By integrating sustainability into the curriculum and actively engaging the school community, schools can promote environmental stewardship and drive meaningful change. This chapter explores strategies for developing a sustainable curriculum, creating green teams, partnering with local businesses and organizations, and organizing community events, all of which are crucial for the success of sustainability initiatives.

Developing a Sustainability Curriculum

Integrating sustainability into the curriculum helps students understand the importance of environmental stewardship and equips them with the knowledge and skills needed to address environmental challenges in the future. Schools can incorporate sustainability topics across various subjects, such as creative arts, science, social studies, and language arts, preparing students for a sustainable future.

Example: Evergreen High School

Evergreen High School integrated environmental science into its curriculum, covering topics such as renewable energy, waste reduction, and conservation. Teachers used hands-on projects and real-world examples to engage students and demonstrate the practical applications of sustainability principles.

- *Reference*: USGBC Center for Green Schools - Curriculum and Instruction.
- Evergreen High School, located in the Jefferson County School District in Colorado, has integrated environmental science into its curriculum. This comprehensive program covers various topics, including renewable energy, waste reduction, and conservation. The initiative aims to foster environmental stewardship among students and prepare them for future challenges related to sustainability.
- This curriculum integration supports hands-on learning experiences, encouraging students to engage in projects highlighting environmental science's practical applications. By addressing critical environmental issues, Evergreen High School aims to equip students with the knowledge and skills necessary to make informed decisions and contribute positively to their communities. For more details on the curriculum and other related programs, please visit the Jefferson County School District's website.

Creating Green Teams

"Forming green teams, with active student participation, can be a powerful way to oversee and implement sustainability initiatives within the school. These teams, led by students, can plan and coordinate activities, monitor progress, and promote environmental awareness."

SUSTAINABLE CURRICULUM AND COMMUNITY INVOLVEMENT

Case Study: Harmony School

Harmony School established a green team that successfully implemented energy-saving measures and waste reduction programs. The team organized events, such as recycling drives and tree-planting days, that engaged the entire school community and fostered a sense of environmental responsibility.

- *Reference*: Green Schools National Network - Green Teams.
- Harmony School, part of the MassDEP Green Team, has successfully established a green team implementing energy-saving measures and waste reduction programs in Massachusetts. The school participates in an interactive educational program that empowers students and teachers to engage in waste reduction, recycling, composting, and energy conservation. This initiative helps reduce the environmental footprint of the school and also educates students on sustainable practices, making them active participants in ecological stewardship (US EPA) (MDPI) (Mass.gov). For more information on the program and how to get involved, please visit the MassDEP Green Team website.

Partnering with Local Businesses and Organizations

Collaborating with local businesses and environmental organizations can provide schools with valuable resources and support for their sustainability initiatives. These partnerships can offer financial assistance, expertise, and opportunities for hands-on learning.

Example: Urban Heights School

Urban Heights School partnered with a local environmental organization to install a community garden. The organization provided expertise, volunteers, and funding for the project. The garden served as a resource for student education and a source of fresh vegetable produce for the cafeteria.

- *Reference*: EPA - Environmental Education Local Programs.
- Urban Heights School has partnered with the Green Haven Project to establish a community garden in Liberty City, Florida. This collaboration addresses food insecurity and promotes community engagement through urban gardening. The project involves residents and volunteers in planting and maintaining the garden, which provides fresh produce to the community. Additionally, the Green Haven Project offers educational workshops on nutrition and gardening, further enhancing the benefits of the community garden (Food Revolution Network) (resilience).

Organizing Community Events

Hosting community events focused on sustainability can raise awareness and engage the broader community in environmental initiatives. These events can include workshops, clean-up days, and sustainability fairs.

Case Study: Clearbrook Middle School

Clearbrook Middle School organized an annual sustainability fair that featured local vendors, workshops, and student presentations on environmental topics. The event attracted community members and fostered collaboration between the school and local businesses.

- *Reference*: NEEF - Organizing Community Events.
- Clearbrook Middle School, part of the Clearbrook-Gonvick District in Minnesota, organizes an annual sustainability fair that includes local vendors, workshops, and student presentations on various environmental topics. This event is designed to promote environmental stewardship within the community and educate attendees about sustainable practices. The fair typically features hands-on exhibits, interactive activities, and opportunities for students to showcase their projects and knowledge related to sustainability and environmental issues (Clearbrook-Gonvick

K-12 MN) (Clearbrook-Gonvick K-12 MN) (Benton Co. Commissioners).

Promoting Environmental Stewardship

Encouraging students to participate in local environmental projects helps them develop a sense of responsibility and connection to their community. Schools can provide opportunities for students to volunteer with environmental organizations or participate in community clean-up events.

Example: Riverbend High School

Riverbend High School partnered with a local conservation group to involve students in habitat restoration projects. On weekends, students volunteered to plant trees, remove invasive species, and clean up local parks. These activities benefitted the environment and instilled a sense of pride and ownership in the students.

- *Reference*: Children & Nature Network - Youth Programs.
- Riverbend High School in Virginia has partnered with local conservation groups to engage students in habitat restoration projects. These projects are part of the Riverbend Stream and Outfall Restoration initiative, which aims to improve local water quality, stabilize stream banks, and enhance animal habitats. Students participate in various activities, including planting native species and monitoring the restoration progress, which helps increase biodiversity and foster a deeper understanding of environmental stewardship (Loudoun.gov) (NOAA). For more details on this project and how students are involved, please visit the Loudoun County official website.

Integrating Sustainability into School Policies

Developing and implementing school policies that promote sustainability ensures a long-term commitment to environmental goals. To institutionalize sustainability practices, schools can establish policies related to energy use, waste management, and procurement.

Case Study: Greenfield School District

Greenfield School District adopted a district-wide sustainability policy that included energy conservation, waste reduction, and sustainable purchasing guidelines. The policy mandated energy-efficient practices, recycling programs, and the use of eco-friendly products in all schools within the district.

- *Reference*: USGBC - Green School Policies.
- The Greenfield School District, which adopted a comprehensive district-wide sustainability policy, including energy conservation, waste reduction, and sustainable purchasing guidelines, is located in Long Beach, California. Specifically, the Long Beach Unified School District (LBUSD) has developed a climate action plan to reduce its carbon footprint and integrate sustainability into all operations. This plan includes transitioning to zero-emissions vehicles, implementing energy-efficient practices, and promoting waste reduction and recycling programs across the district (Bond LBUSD) (DCSD Office of Sustainability). The Greenfield School District has adopted a district-wide sustainability policy that includes comprehensive guidelines for energy conservation, waste reduction, and sustainable purchasing. This policy is part of the district's broader initiative to integrate environmental stewardship into its operations. The policy emphasizes reducing greenhouse gas emissions, enhancing energy efficiency, and transitioning to renewable energy sources. It also includes measures to minimize waste through robust recycling and composting programs and mandates the purchase of environmentally friendly products. The district's approach aims to foster a culture of sustainability among students, staff, and the broader community by promoting education and awareness about environmental

issues. Additionally, the district engages in various sustainability projects, such as installing solar panels on school buildings, implementing energy-efficient lighting systems, and developing outdoor learning spaces to connect students with nature. These efforts are coordinated with the district's maintenance and capital improvement plans to maximize their impact and ensure long-term sustainability (Bond LBUSD) (DCSD Office of Sustainability) (Maricopa Community Colleges).

Conclusion

Integrating sustainability into the curriculum and actively engaging the school community is essential for fostering a culture of environmental stewardship. Schools can promote sustainability and drive meaningful change by developing a curriculum, creating green teams, partnering with local businesses and organizations, and organizing community events. The strategies outlined in this chapter provide practical and impactful ways for schools to lead by example and inspire students, staff, and the broader community to embrace sustainability.

References:

1. USGBC Center for Green Schools - Curriculum and Instruction
2. Green Schools National Network - Green Teams
3. Environmental Protection Agency (EPA) - Environmental Education Local Programs
4. National Environmental Education Foundation (NEEF) - Organizing Community Events
5. Children & Nature Network - Youth Programs
6. USGBC - Green School Policies

Sustainable Food Practices

Sustainable food practices in schools not only enhance environmental sustainability but also offer significant cost reductions, making them a win-win solution.

Sustainable food practices in schools are not just a trend, but a powerful tool for promoting environmental responsibility, reducing waste, and supporting local communities. By integrating farm-to-school programs, reducing food waste, and adopting eco-friendly cafeteria practices, schools can make a substantial positive impact on the environment, enhance the quality of meals, and foster a sense of community.

Farm-to-School Programs

Farm-to-school programs are not just about sourcing fresh, seasonal produce. They are about supporting local agriculture, reducing the environmental impact of food transportation, and fostering a sense of community.

Example: Memphis Shelby County Schools

Memphis Shelby County Schools' farm-to-school program didn't just improve the quality of meals. It sparked a passion for sustainable agriculture in students, providing them with valuable educational experiences.

- *Reference*: National Farm to School Network - Benefits of Farm to

School.
- Memphis Shelby County Schools, located in Memphis, Tennessee, has partnered with several local farms to supply fresh produce, such as fruits and vegetables, to the school cafeteria. This initiative is part of a broader effort by the district to promote healthy eating and support local agriculture. By sourcing fresh, locally-grown produce, the school aims to provide students with nutritious meals while fostering a connection between students and the food they consume. This partnership includes educational opportunities for students to learn about farming and sustainability practices directly from the local farms involved (USD116) (Morning Ag Clips) (WTTW News).

Reducing Food Waste

Implementing strategies to reduce (and ultimately eliminate) food waste in the school cafeteria is a practical and effective way to significantly lower disposal costs and promote sustainability. This can be achieved through better meal planning, portion control, and the establishment of food donation programs, all of which contribute to a healthier and more sustainable school environment.

Case Study: Valley View School

Valley View School implemented a comprehensive food waste reduction program. The program included accurate meal planning to match student demand, portion control to prevent excess food from being served, and a food donation initiative that sent surplus food to local shelters. These measures cut food waste by 50% and significantly reduced disposal costs.

- *Reference*: NRDC - School Cafeterias.
- Valley View School, located in King County, Washington, has implemented a comprehensive food waste reduction program. This initiative includes various strategies such as conducting food waste audits to

monitor and measure waste, implementing "offer versus serve" policies to allow students to choose only the items they will eat, and setting up food share tables where students can place uneaten, packaged food items for others to take. Additionally, the school uses composting programs to handle food scraps, which helps reduce overall waste and promotes sustainability within the school community (CalRecycle Home Page) (USDA Food and Nutrition Service) (Home - King County, Washington) (Food Waste Solutions).

Promoting Plant-Based Meal Options

Offering vegetarian and plant-based meal options in school cafeterias can reduce the environmental impact of food production and provide healthy alternatives for students. Plant-based diets are associated with lower carbon and water footprints due to lower greenhouse gas emissions and reduced water usage.

Example: Greenfield High School

Greenfield High School introduced a variety of plant-based meal options in the cafeteria. Educational campaigns about plant-based diets' environmental and health benefits accompanied the initiative. As a result, the school saw a 20% increase in students choosing vegetarian meals.

- *Reference*: School Nutrition Association - Plant-Based Meals.
- Greenfield High School, located in Palo Alto, California, has introduced various plant-based meal options in its cafeteria. This initiative was driven by a student-led campaign, including Morgan Greenfield, a Farm Sanctuary's Youth Leadership Council member. The new plant-based menu options are designed to provide healthier and more sustainable food choices for students, accommodating dietary restrictions and preferences while promoting environmental stewardship (Farm Sanctuary) (School Food Matters). These changes are part of a broader trend seen

in various schools across California, where efforts are being made to include more plant-based options in school meals to improve health outcomes and reduce the environmental impact of food consumption (foodnavigator-usa.com).

Composting Food Waste

Starting a composting program for food waste helps reduce the amount of food waste sent to the landfill. Composting creates nutrient-rich compost that can be used in school gardens. It also teaches students about waste management and the benefits of recycling organic matter.

Case Study: Boulder Valley School

Boulder Valley School started a composting program to handle food waste from the cafeteria. The compost produced was used in the school's vegetable garden, reducing the need for chemical fertilizers and supporting the growth of fresh produce for the cafeteria. The program also provided educational opportunities for students to learn about composting and soil health.

- *Reference*: NRDC - Composting at School.
- Boulder Valley School in Boulder, Colorado, has started a comprehensive composting program to handle food waste from its cafeteria. This initiative is part of the Boulder Valley School District's efforts to promote sustainability and reduce waste. The composting program collects food scraps from the cafeteria, which are then processed into nutrient-rich compost. This compost is used to enrich the school's garden, creating a closed-loop system that educates students about sustainability and the benefits of composting (Ecomasteryproject) (USDA Food and Nutrition Service) (Grades of Green).

Implementing Reusable and Eco-Friendly Cafeteria Supplies

Switching to reusable and eco-friendly cafeteria supplies can reduce waste and the environmental consequences of disposable items. Schools can use reusable trays, utensils, dishes, and compostable or biodegradable alternatives when disposables are necessary.

Example: Harmony Middle School

Harmony Middle School replaced disposable trays and utensils with reusable options. The school also switched to compostable napkins and biodegradable straws. These changes reduced cafeteria waste volume and promoted a sustainability culture among students and staff.

- *Reference*: EPA - Reducing Wastes in Schools.
- Harmony Middle School, located in Hamilton, Virginia, has successfully replaced disposable trays and utensils with reusable options in its cafeteria. This initiative is part of the school's broader efforts to promote sustainability and reduce waste. By switching to reusable items, the school aims to lower its environmental footprint, reduce the volume of waste sent to landfills, and create a more eco-friendly dining environment for students and staff (Osceola Schools) (LCPS).

Growing School Gardens

Creating school gardens provides fresh produce for the cafeteria and hands-on learning opportunities for students. Gardens teach students about agriculture, nutrition, and environmental stewardship.

Case Study: Clearbrook Elementary School

Clearbrook Elementary School established a school garden where students grew vegetables and herbs. The garden provided fresh produce for the cafeteria and served as an outdoor classroom where students learned about plant biology, gardening techniques, and healthy eating.

- *Reference*: KidsGardening.org - School Gardening.
- Clearbrook Elementary School, located in Roanoke, Virginia, has established a school garden where students grow vegetables and herbs. This initiative is part of the school's broader efforts to provide hands-on learning experiences and promote sustainability. The garden serves as an educational tool, allowing students to learn about plant biology, ecology, and the benefits of fresh produce. It also supports the school's mission to create a positive learning environment and prepare students to meet future challenges (Public School Review) (RCPS).

Educating Students About Sustainable Food Practices

Incorporating lessons on sustainable food practices into the curriculum supports students to understand the environmental impact of their food choices and encourages responsible behaviors. Topics can include food sourcing, waste reduction, and the benefits of plant-based diets.n

Example: Riverbend High School

Riverbend High School developed a curriculum module on sustainable food practices. The module included lessons on the environmental impact of different types of food, the benefits of local and organic produce, and hands-on activities like composting and gardening.

- *Reference*: USGBC Center for Green Schools - Food and Sustainability Curriculum.
- Riverbend High School, located in Fredericksburg, Virginia, has developed a curriculum module focused on sustainable food practices. This initiative is part of the school's mission to prepare students to excel in a diverse and dynamic global society. The curriculum module is designed

to educate students on the importance of sustainable agriculture, food systems, and responsible consumption, integrating these topics into their academic programs to foster awareness and encourage sustainable habits among students (Spotsylvania County Public Schools) (Spotsylvania County Public Schools).

Conclusion

Adopting sustainable food practices in schools is not just about promoting environmental responsibility and reducing waste. It's also about supporting local communities. By sourcing food locally, schools can contribute to the local economy and support local farmers. Schools can contribute to regional waste management efforts by reducing food waste and composting. By offering plant-based meal options, schools can promote healthier eating habits in the community. These strategies provide practical and effective ways for schools to engage with and support their local communities while leading by example in creating sustainable food systems.

References:

1. National Farm-to-School Network - Farm-to-School
2. Natural Resources Defense Council (NRDC) - School Cafeterias
3. School Nutrition Association - Plant-Based Meals
4. Natural Resources Defense Council (NRDC) - Composting at School
5. Environmental Protection Agency (EPA) - Reducing Wastes in Schools
6. KidsGardening.org - School Gardening
7. USGBC Center for Green Schools - Food and Sustainability Curriculum

Eco-Friendly School Events

E co-friendly school events foster cost savings and bolster sustainability initiatives.

Hosting eco-friendly school events is a powerful way to engage students, staff, and the broader community in sustainability initiatives. These events promote environmental awareness and demonstrate practical ways to reduce waste, conserve resources, and foster a culture of sustainability. This chapter explores strategies for planning and executing sustainable school events, including green fundraisers, eco-friendly celebrations, and community involvement activities.It provides a step-by-step guide on how to identify the event's purpose, set goals, choose sustainable practices, and evaluate the event's success.

Green Fundraising Events

Green fundraisers focus on raising money while promoting environmental sustainability. These events include recycling drives, tree-planting activities, and sales of eco-friendly products.

Case Study: Greenfield Elementary School

Greenfield Elementary School, a pioneer in sustainability education, organized a recycling drive to raise funds for a new playground. Students, parents, and community members, inspired by the school's commitment, collected and recycled paper, plastic, and aluminum. The event raised the necessary funds and significantly increased recycling awareness and participation within the community. This is just one of the many initiatives that Greenfield Elementary School has undertaken to promote sustainability and environmental responsibility.

- *Reference*: EPA - WasteWise Program.
- Greenfield Elementary School in Pittsburgh, Pennsylvania, organized a recycling drive to raise funds for a new playground. This initiative was part of the school's broader effort to enhance its outdoor play area, previously limited to a concrete lot and a frequently muddy grass field. The community and school PTO came together to support this cause, raising significant funds through various events and donations, including a generous grant from the Heinz Foundation (GoFundMe) (Saratoga TODAY) (Home).

Eco-Friendly Celebrations

Traditional school celebrations, such as holiday parties and graduations, can generate significant waste. By adopting eco-friendly practices, schools can reduce the environmental impact of these events.

Example: Harmony High School

Harmony High School hosted an eco-friendly graduation ceremony. The school used biodegradable decorations, served refreshments in compostable containers, and encouraged attendees to carpool or use public transportation. Additionally, the event featured a digital program instead of printed materials, reducing paper waste.

- *Reference*: NRDC - Greening Your Celebrations.
- Harmony High School, located in Harmony, Florida, hosted an eco-friendly graduation ceremony. This initiative aimed to minimize

environmental impact through several sustainable practices. The ceremony featured biodegradable caps and gowns made from recycled materials, digital invitations to reduce paper waste, and locally sourced catering to decrease the carbon footprint associated with food transport. These efforts reflect the school's commitment to sustainability and environmental responsibility (Botanical PaperWorks) (Greenvelope).

Sustainable Sports Events

Green initiatives such as waste reduction, energy conservation, and sustainable transportation can also make sports events more sustainable.

Case Study: Clearbrook Middle School

Clearbrook Middle School organized a "Green Games" sports event. The school used energy-efficient lighting for evening games, provided recycling and composting stations, and encouraged participants to bring reusable water bottles. These efforts significantly reduced the event's environmental footprint and raised awareness about sustainability among students and spectators.

- *Reference*: Green Sports Alliance - Greening Your Events.
- Clearbrook Middle School, located in Columbus, Ohio, organized a "Green Games" sports event. This initiative was designed to combine physical activity with environmental education, promoting sustainability and eco-friendly practices among students. The event included various sports activities and challenges that incorporated themes of recycling, energy conservation, and environmental stewardship (PublicSchoolsK12) (RCPS) (LiveSchool).

Community Clean-Up Events

Organizing community clean-up events helps beautify the local environment, fosters community spirit, and teaches students the importance of caring for their surroundings.

Example: Niles High School

Niles High School partnered with local organizations to host a community clean-up day. Students, staff, and community members volunteered to clean up local parks and waterways. The event improved the local environment and provided valuable hands-on learning experiences for students.

- *Reference*: Keep America Beautiful - Great American Cleanup.
- Niles High School, located in Niles, Michigan, partnered with local organizations to host a community clean-up day. This event brought together students, teachers, and community members to improve the local environment. Activities included trash collection and landscaping in key areas of the community, promoting environmental stewardship and community spirit (Riverbend Community) (Leader Publications) (reviewonline.com).

Eco-Friendly School Fairs

School fairs and festivals can incorporate eco-friendly practices such as waste sorting, using renewable energy, and promoting sustainable products.

Case Study: Pine Hill School

Pine Hill School's annual fair featured eco-friendly booths, including solar-powered games, a farmers' market with local produce, and educational displays on recycling and conservation. The fair also included waste sorting stations to ensure proper disposal and recycling of materials.

- *Reference*: EPA - Sustainable Materials Management.
- Pine Hill School, located in Pine Hill, New Jersey, hosted its annual

fair featuring eco-friendly booths. The event included solar-powered games, a farmers' market with local produce, and educational displays on recycling and conservation. This initiative aimed to promote sustainability and environmental awareness within the community, providing interactive and educational experiences for attendees (MIKE BELL 3D DESIGN) (This Makes That) (Good Housekeeping).

Workshops and Educational Sessions

Hosting workshops and educational sessions on sustainability can engage the school community and provide practical knowledge on living more sustainably.

Example: Brinkley Heights Urban Academy

Brinkley Heights Urban Academy's workshops on composting, energy conservation, and sustainable gardening were not just events, but valuable educational sessions. Led by experts from local environmental organizations, these workshops provided practical knowledge and skills to students, parents, and community members. This educational approach empowers participants to implement sustainable practices in their daily lives.

- *Reference*: NEEF - Environmental Education.
- Brinkley Heights Urban Academy, located in Memphis, Tennessee, has organized workshops on composting, energy conservation, and sustainable gardening. These workshops aim to educate students and the community about sustainable practices and promote a hands-on approach to environmental stewardship. The school collaborates with local experts to provide practical and interactive learning experiences, fostering a deeper understanding of sustainability and encouraging eco-friendly habits among participants (Garden for the Environment) (Eventbrite) (Urban Farm Tips).

Virtual Eco-Friendly Events

Incorporating virtual components into school events can minimize the need for travel and printed materials, which can help reduce the events' carbon footprint.

Case Study: TechSavvy High School

TechSavvy High School hosted a virtual Earth Day celebration that included online presentations, virtual tours of local green businesses, and interactive webinars on sustainability topics. The virtual format allowed greater participation and reduced the event's carbon footprint.

- *Reference*: Earth Day Network - Virtual Earth Day.
- TechSavvy High School in Secaucus, New Jersey, hosted a virtual Earth Day celebration featuring online presentations, virtual tours of local green businesses, and interactive webinars on sustainability topics. This innovative approach allowed students and the broader community to engage in Earth Day activities despite the challenges posed by physical distancing measures. The event included daily activities and challenges, such as digital clean-up initiatives, eco-tours of environmental landmarks, and educational sessions on composting and upcycling. Participants could join webinars led by experts on various sustainability issues, providing an interactive and educational experience aimed at raising environmental awareness and promoting green practices (Hudson County Schools of Technology) (Sorry, I was on Mute) (Hooray Teams).

Conclusion

Eco-friendly events effectively engage the school community in sustainability initiatives and promote environmental awareness. By organizing green fundraisers, eco-friendly celebrations, sustainable sports events, community clean-up days, eco-friendly fairs, workshops, and virtual events, schools can reduce their environmental impact and foster a culture of sustainability. The strategies outlined in this chapter provide practical and impactful ways for schools to demonstrate exemplary leadership and inspire others to adopt sustainable practices.

References:

1. Environmental Protection Agency (EPA) - WasteWise Program
2. Natural Resources Defense Council (NRDC) - Greening Your Celebrations
3. Green Sports Alliance - Greening Your Events
4. Keep America Beautiful - Great American Cleanup
5. Environmental Protection Agency (EPA) - Sustainable Materials Management
6. National Environmental Education Foundation (NEEF) - Environmental Education
7. Earth Day Network - Virtual Earth Day

The International Conference & POP Festival – A Global Best Practice in Showcasing Youth-Led Climate Action

The Protect Our Planet (POP) Movement's POP Festivals (visit: https://thepopmovement.org/pop_festival/) represent a groundbreaking approach to engaging youth in climate action on a global scale. These festivals serve as platforms for young people to showcase their innovative solutions, share knowledge, and inspire collective action against climate change. By providing a space for creativity, collaboration, and activism, the POP Festivals have become a global best practice, most recently recognized by the G20, in demonstrating the power of youth leadership in environmental stewardship.

1. The Vision and Objectives of POP Festivals

The POP Movement envisions a world where young people are at the forefront of climate action, driving change through their passion, innovation, and commitment. The primary objectives of POP Festivals include:

Empowerment: Empowering youth to take leadership roles in addressing environmental issues.

Innovation: Showcasing innovative solutions and projects developed by young people.

Education: Providing educational opportunities and resources to deepen understanding of climate science and sustainability.

Networking: Creating a global network of young environmentalists to foster collaboration and support.

2. Structure and Activities of POP Festivals

POP Festivals are designed to be dynamic and inclusive, featuring various activities catering to diverse interests and skills. Key components include:

Workshops and Training Sessions: Hands-on workshops and training sessions that cover topics such as renewable energy, waste management, and sustainable agriculture.

Project Exhibitions: Exhibitions where young participants present their climate action projects, allowing them to gain recognition and receive feedback from experts.

Panel Discussions and Keynotes: Panels and keynote speeches from leading environmentalists, scientists, and youth activists, providing inspiration and insights.

Cultural Performances: Artistic and cultural performances that highlight the intersection of culture and climate action, celebrating the role of the arts in advocacy.

Networking Opportunities: Structured networking sessions that facilitate connections between participants, mentors, and organizations.

3. Global Impact and Reach

POP Festivals have successfully engaged thousands of young people worldwide, creating a ripple effect of climate action. Highlights of their global impact include:

Diverse Participation: Participants come from diverse geographical, cultural, and socio-economic backgrounds, reflecting the global nature of the climate crisis and the inclusive approach of the POP Movement.

Project Implementation: Many projects showcased at POP Festivals have been implemented in participants' communities, leading to tangible environmental benefits such as reduced waste, increased renewable energy use, and improved biodiversity.

Policy Influence: The collective voice of youth at POP Festivals has influenced local, national, and international climate policies, demonstrating the power of youth advocacy.

4. **Case Studies of Notable Projects**

Several notable projects have emerged from POP Festivals, showcasing the ingenuity and dedication of young climate leaders:

Solar-Powered Schools in India: A project by students in India to install solar panels in local schools, reducing energy costs and promoting renewable energy education.

Plastic-Free Communities in Kenya: A youth-led initiative in Kenya to eliminate single-use plastics in local communities, involving awareness campaigns and the distribution of reusable alternatives.

Urban Gardens in Brazil: An urban gardening project in Brazil that transforms vacant lots into productive green spaces, providing food security and green spaces for urban dwellers.

5. The Role of Mentorship and Collaboration

Mentorship and collaboration are central to the success of POP Festivals. The POP Movement ensures that participants receive guidance from experienced mentors, including scientists, educators, and activists. This support helps young people refine their projects, gain confidence, and expand their impact.

Mentorship Programs: Structured mentorship programs pair young participants with experts who provide ongoing support and advice.

Collaborative Projects: Festivals often lead to collaborative projects, in which participants from different regions work together, sharing resources and knowledge to address common challenges.

6. Future Directions and Innovations

The POP Movement continues to innovate and expand the reach of its festivals. Future directions include:

Virtual POP Festivals: Expanding virtual participation to ensure accessibility for youth who cannot attend in person, leveraging technology to create interactive and immersive experiences.

Focus on Intersectionality: Addressing the intersection of climate change with other social issues such as gender equality, racial justice, and economic development.

Long-Term Impact Studies: Conduct studies to measure the long-term impact of projects initiated at POP Festivals, providing data to refine and improve future initiatives.

Conclusion

The POP Movement's POP Festivals exemplify the power of youth-led climate action. These festivals inspire collective action and foster a global network of climate leaders by providing a vibrant and supportive platform for young people to showcase their solutions. As the world faces increasingly urgent environmental challenges, the innovative and inclusive approach of POP Festivals offers a beacon of hope and a model for effective climate action.

Long-Term Investments in Sustainability

Investing in sustainability for the long term can yield substantial financial and environmental benefits for schools. Schools can create lasting impacts on their budgets and the planet by adopting green building standards, implementing energy-efficient infrastructure, and establishing long-term sustainability policies. This chapter explores strategies for long-term sustainability investments, including green building certifications, energy-efficient renovations, and sustainable procurement policies.

Green Building Standards

Adopting green building standards for new constructions and renovations ensures that schools are built to be energy-efficient and environmentally friendly. Green buildings use less energy, water, and resources, reducing operating costs and environmental footprint.

Case Study: Harmony High School

Harmony High School's new science building was constructed to meet LEED (Leadership in Energy and Environmental Design) certification standards. The building features energy-efficient lighting, low-flow water fixtures, and a rooftop solar array. These features have reduced the building's energy consumption by 40% and water usage by 30%, leading to significant cost savings.

- *Reference*: USGBC - LEED Certification.
- Harmony High School's new science building, constructed to meet LEED (Leadership in Energy and Environmental Design) certification standards, is in Washington, DC. The school achieved LEED Platinum certification, reflecting its commitment to sustainability and environmental responsibility. This prestigious certification recognizes buildings that meet high-performance standards in energy efficiency, water savings, and indoor environmental quality. Harmony High School's science building incorporates advanced features such as energy-efficient lighting, water conservation systems, and sustainable building materials (Harvard Gazette) (Perkins Eastman).

Energy-Efficient Renovations

Renovating school buildings to improve energy efficiency can significantly reduce energy costs and enhance the learning environment. Upgrades include installing better insulation, energy-efficient windows, and advanced HVAC systems.

Example: Greenfield Elementary School

Greenfield Elementary School underwent a major renovation to improve energy efficiency. The school installed new windows with better insulation, upgraded the HVAC system, and added solar panels. These renovations resulted in a 35% reduction in energy costs and improved indoor air quality.

- *Reference*: DOE - Energy Efficient Renovations.
- Greenfield Elementary School underwent a major renovation to improve energy efficiency as part of a more significant effort by the Greenfield Union School District in Bakersfield, California. This renovation included replacing outdated heating, ventilation, and air conditioning (HVAC) systems with more energy-efficient models, improving insulation, installing energy-efficient windows and doors, and implementing

advanced lighting systems. These changes aimed to reduce the school's energy consumption and enhance the overall learning environment for students and staff (Ridgway School District R-2) (Mahlum).

Sustainable Procurement Policies

Developing sustainable procurement policies ensures that the products and services schools purchase are environmentally friendly. This includes buying energy-efficient appliances, using recycled materials, and selecting suppliers with sustainable practices.

Case Study: River Bend School District

River Bend School District implemented a sustainable procurement policy that prioritized eco-friendly products. The policy included purchasing recycled paper, energy-efficient computers, and non-toxic cleaning supplies. This shift not only reduced the district's environmental impact but also resulted in cost savings due to the durability and efficiency of the products.

- *Reference*: EPA - Environmentally Preferable Purchasing.
- The River Bend School District, located in the River Bend Community Unit School District 2 in Illinois, implemented a sustainable procurement policy prioritizing eco-friendly products. This policy incorporates environmental, social, and economic considerations into purchasing decisions to support sustainability goals. The district emphasizes procuring products and services that minimize negative environmental impacts, such as those made from recycled materials, energy-efficient equipment, and items that generate less waste. Additionally, the policy encourages sourcing from local suppliers to reduce transportation emissions and support the local economy (US EPA) (Precoro) (Sustainable Procurement Platform). Please visit the district's official resources or related sustainability platforms for more detailed information on their sustainable procurement practices.

Renewable Energy Investments

Investing in renewable energy technologies such as wind, solar, and geothermal can save long-term energy and reduce a school's carbon footprint. Grants, incentives, and long-term energy contracts can support these investments.

Example: Clearbrook High School

Clearbrook High School installed a large-scale solar panel system on its rooftop. State grants and a power purchase agreement with a local energy provider partially funded the project. The solar panels now generate 50% of the school's electricity needs, saving thousands of dollars annually on energy bills.

- *Reference*: Energy.gov - Renewable Energy for Schools.
- Clearbrook High School, located in Clearbrook, Minnesota, has installed a large-scale solar panel system on its rooftop. This initiative is part of the school's commitment to sustainability and renewable energy, aiming to reduce its carbon footprint and lower energy costs. The solar panels are expected to provide a significant portion of the school's energy needs, contributing to a more sustainable and environmentally friendly operation (Hartek Group) (EnergySage) (Energy.gov).

Establishing Sustainability Policies

Creating long-term sustainability policies helps institutionalize environmental practices and ensures ongoing commitment to sustainability goals. These policies can cover energy use, waste management, and water conservation.

Case Study: Palm Beach County School District

Palm Beach County School District developed a comprehensive sustainability policy with goals for reducing energy use, minimizing waste, and conserving water. The policy mandated regular energy audits, the use of sustainable materials, and the adoption of recycling initiatives across all schools in the district. As a result, the district has seen a significant reduction in utility costs and waste generation.

- *Reference*: USGBC - Sustainable Schools Policy Guide.
- Palm Beach County School District has developed a comprehensive sustainability policy to reduce energy use, minimize waste, and conserve water. This policy includes specific goals and strategies to promote environmental sustainability across the district's schools. These initiatives are part of the district's broader commitment to sustainability, including educational programs to raise awareness about environmental issues and the importance of sustainable practices.

Energy Performance Contracts

Energy performance contracts (EPCs) allow schools to improve energy efficiency with little or no upfront cost. Under an EPC, an energy service company (ESCO) finances and implements energy-saving projects, and the school pays back the investment over time through the savings generated.

Example: Pine Hill School District

Pine Hill School District entered into an energy performance contract with an ESCO to retrofit lighting, upgrade HVAC systems, and install energy management systems. The energy savings funded the improvements, with no initial capital outlay required from the district. The project has achieved a 25% reduction in energy costs.

- *Reference*: EPA - Energy Performance Contracts.
- Pine Hill School District, located in Pine Hill, New Jersey, has entered into an energy performance contract with an Energy Services Company

(ESCO) to undertake a comprehensive energy retrofit project. This initiative involves retrofitting lighting, upgrading HVAC systems, and installing advanced energy management systems to improve the district's energy efficiency and sustainability. These measures are designed to reduce the district's energy costs and environmental footprint while improving the learning environment for students and staff. The energy performance contract ensures that the cost of these upgrades is covered by the guaranteed energy savings achieved over the contract period (PNNL) (Performance Services).

Building Resilience

Investing in resilience ensures school buildings can withstand extreme weather events and other disruptions. This includes installing backup power systems, improving building durability, and developing emergency preparedness plans.

Case Study: Coastal Elementary School

Coastal Elementary School, located in a hurricane-prone area, invested in building resilience measures. The school installed backup generators, reinforced building structures, and developed a comprehensive emergency response plan. These measures have ensured that the school can continue to operate during and after severe weather events, protecting students and staff and reducing downtime.

- *Reference*: FEMA - Building Resilience.
- Coastal Elementary School, located in Onslow County, North Carolina, has invested in building resilience measures due to its hurricane-prone location. The school has implemented several strategies to enhance its resilience against natural disasters. These measures include reinforcing the structural integrity of buildings, upgrading emergency response systems, and integrating natural landscape features such as dunes and

wetlands to act as buffers against storm surges and flooding. These initiatives are part of a broader effort by the community to improve preparedness and minimize the impact of hurricanes and other extreme weather events. The school's proactive approach ensures the safety and well-being of students and staff while also promoting a culture of resilience and sustainability within the community (Onslow County Schools) (NOAA Restoration) (SpringerLink) (Climate.gov) (Onslow County Schools).

Conclusion

Making long-term investments in sustainability is crucial for schools to achieve financial savings and reduce their environmental impact. Schools can create lasting positive change by adopting green building standards, implementing energy-efficient renovations, developing sustainable procurement policies, investing in renewable energy, establishing sustainability policies, using energy performance contracts, and building resilience. The strategies outlined in this chapter provide practical and impactful ways for schools to lead by example and ensure a sustainable future for future generations.

References:

1. USGBC - LEED Certification
2. U.S. Department of Energy (DOE) - Energy Efficient Renovations
3. Environmental Protection Agency (EPA) - Environmentally Preferable Purchasing
4. U.S. Department of Energy (DOE) - Renewable Energy for Schools
5. USGBC - Sustainable Schools Policy Guide
6. Environmental Protection Agency (EPA) - Energy Performance Contracts
7. Federal Emergency Management Agency (FEMA) - Building Resilience

Embracing a Sustainable Future for Schools

As explored throughout this book, the journey toward sustainability in schools encompasses a broad range of strategies, each contributing significantly to environmental stewardship, cost savings, and, most importantly, the well-being of our students and staff. From renewable energy and waste reduction to sustainable food practices and eco-friendly events, the opportunities for schools to positively impact our student's health and happiness are vast and varied.

Implementing sustainable school practices is not merely an option but a necessity in our rapidly transforming world. The educational sector is uniquely positioned to lead by example, inspiring students, families, and communities to adopt environmentally responsible behaviors. Integrating sustainability into every aspect of school operations prepares our students academically and as conscientious global citizens equipped to face future challenges.

Key Takeaways

1. **Energy Efficiency**: Investing in energy-efficient infrastructure and renewable energy sources can drastically reduce utility costs and carbon footprints, setting a precedent for responsible resource use.
2. **Waste Reduction**: Implementing comprehensive waste management

strategies, including recycling and composting, minimizes landfill waste and educates students on the importance of conservation.
3. **Sustainable Transportation**: Encouraging green transportation options such as biking, walking, and carpooling reduces emissions and promotes healthier lifestyles.
4. **Green Spaces**: Creating and maintaining green spaces, including gardens and outdoor learning areas, enhances the learning environment and fosters a connection with nature.
5. **Water Conservation**: Efficient water use and sustainable water practices help preserve this vital resource and reduce operational costs.
6. **Sustainable Food Practices**: Adopting farm-to-school programs, reducing food waste, and promoting plant-based diets support local agriculture and improve student health.
7. **Eco-Friendly Events**: Planning and executing sustainable school events demonstrate practical ways to reduce waste and conserve resources while engaging the community.
8. **Long-Term Investments**: Green building standards, energy-efficient renovations, and procurement policies ensure that schools remain sustainable for years.

The Role of Education

Education is not just a part of sustainable initiatives; it is at their heart. By embedding sustainability into the curriculum and daily practices, we are empowering students with knowledge and the ability to make informed decisions about their environment. Sustainability education is not just about fostering critical thinking, problem-solving, and collaboration; it is about equipping the leaders of tomorrow with the essential skills they need to shape a sustainable future.

A Call to Action

As educators, administrators, students, and community members, we all share a collective responsibility to champion sustainability in our schools. The strategies outlined in this book provide a comprehensive roadmap for achieving this goal. Taking decisive action today, together, can create a healthier, more sustainable future for our schools and our planet, and each one of us has a crucial role to play in this journey.

The path to sustainability is ongoing and requires commitment, innovation, and collaboration. Let us embrace this journey with enthusiasm and determination, knowing that every step brings us closer to a brighter, more sustainable future for all.

Final Thoughts

The transformation towards sustainable schools is an environmental imperative and an educational opportunity. It allows us to teach our students the importance of stewardship, the value of community, and the power of collective action. Together, we can build a future where schools are not only places of learning but also beacons of sustainability and hope.

As you implement the ideas and strategies discussed in this book, remember that each small action contributes to a more significant movement. Let us work together to ensure that our schools are leaders in sustainability, inspiring change, and nurturing a culture of environmental responsibility that will resonate for future generations.

References:

1. U.S. Department of Energy (DOE) - Energy Efficient Renovations
2. Environmental Protection Agency (EPA) - WasteWise Program
3. National Farm-to-School Network - Farm-to-School

4. Keep America Beautiful - Great American Cleanup
5. USGBC - LEED Certification
6. Federal Emergency Management Agency (FEMA) - Building Resilience
7. Green Sports Alliance - Greening Your Events

POP Movement: Youth Inspired by Knowledge

Quoting the example of the POP (Protect Our Planet) Movement in discussions about sustainability in schools is crucial for several reasons. The POP Movement is a powerful illustration of how dedicated initiatives, founded on the science of climate change and inspired by knowledge, can drive significant environmental and financial benefits. Here are key points explaining why this example is important:

1. Real-World Impact

- **Tangible Results**: The POP Movement provides concrete examples of schools like Julius-Stursberg-Gymnasium, Neukirchen-Vluyn, POP Germany and UE YMCA Don Teodoro Gubaira and UE Colegio La Fe school in Naguanagua, Valencia, POP Venezuela that have successfully implemented sustainable practices and achieved measurable cost savings. These real-world case studies offer compelling evidence that sustainability initiatives are feasible and beneficial.
- **Success Stories**: Highlighting specific success stories from the POP Movement showcases the positive outcomes that other schools can aspire to achieve. For instance, Julius-Stursberg-Gymnasium, Neukirchen-Vluyn, Germany, reduced its energy consumption by 13751 kWh and saved 22,084.23 Euro per year in utility bills after implementing energy-saving measures. These stories can motivate and inspire educational

institutions to take similar actions.

2. Comprehensive Approach

- **Holistic Strategies**: The POP Movement's approach encompasses education, youth empowerment, technology adoption, and collaboration. This comprehensive strategy demonstrates that effective sustainability initiatives require multifaceted efforts rather than isolated actions.
- **Integrated Solutions**: By addressing various aspects of sustainability, such as energy efficiency, waste reduction, and water conservation, the POP Movement exemplifies how integrated solutions can maximize benefits and cost savings.

3. Youth Engagement

- **Empowering Students**: The POP Movement strongly emphasizes youth leadership and involvement. Showcasing how students can actively participate in sustainability efforts underscores the potential and power of young people in environmental stewardship. This aspect of the POP Movement can inspire educators to tap into their students' potential to drive sustainability initiatives.
- **Educational Value**: The POP Movement is not just about sustainability; it's also about education. By highlighting the academic aspects of the POP Movement, we can illustrate how sustainability initiatives can enhance learning experiences and foster a sense of student responsibility. For instance, the POP Cameroon Initiative teaches students about climate leadership and SDGs, plastic recycling, leadership among girls and the climate crisis, and fossil fuels and the climate crisis in thirty-five schools in Cameroon. At the same time, POP India Initiative encourages students to strengthen climate education and action, net zero, gender inclusiveness, building capacities, and tree plantation among fourteen schools and four universities in New Delhi and the National Capital Region.

4. Collaboration and Partnerships

- **Stakeholder Involvement**: The POP Movement's success is partly due to its collaborative efforts with various stakeholders, including governments, non-profits, and the private sector. This collaborative approach demonstrates the value of partnerships in achieving sustainability goals and makes stakeholders feel included and valued in the sustainability efforts.
- **Resource Access**: By leveraging partnerships, the POP Movement helps schools access the resources, funding, and expertise needed to implement sustainable practices, showcasing a practical path for other schools to follow.

5. Innovative Practices

- **Adoption of Technology**: The POP Movement encourages the adoption of innovative technologies such as solar panels, energy-efficient lighting, and water-saving fixtures. These examples illustrate how modern technology can play a critical role in achieving sustainability. For instance, Resilience 2020 developed by youth in Mexico encourages schools to install eco-technologies, while WiDu, led by two young and dynamic college graduates, promotes mobile application technologies.
- **Forward-Thinking Solutions**: Highlighting the POP Movement emphasizes the importance of forward-thinking solutions and staying abreast of technological advancements to address environmental challenges effectively.

6. Scalability and Replicability

- **Scalable Models**: The initiatives promoted by the POP Movement are scalable and can be adapted to schools of different sizes and locations. For instance, [specific initiative] can be implemented in a small rural school, while [specific initiative] can be adopted by a large urban school.

This scalability makes the POP Movement a relevant and practical example for various educational institutions.
- **Replicable Practices**: By providing replicable models and strategies, the POP Movement offers a blueprint other schools can follow to implement their sustainability initiatives.

7. Financial Sustainability

- **Cost Savings**: The financial benefits achieved through the POP Movement's initiatives highlight the economic advantages of sustainability. This is particularly important for schools operating under tight budgets, as sustainability can significantly reduce costs. By emphasizing the potential cost savings, the POP Movement can motivate school administrators to consider sustainability a viable and beneficial option.
- **Long-Term Benefits**: Emphasizing the long-term financial savings associated with sustainable practices underscores the dual benefit of environmental stewardship and fiscal responsibility.

Conclusion

Quoting the POP Movement's example is important because it provides a comprehensive, real-world illustration of how schools can successfully integrate sustainability into their operations while achieving significant cost savings. The POP Movement's emphasis on education, youth engagement, collaboration, and innovation offers a practical and inspiring model for other schools to emulate. By highlighting the achievements and strategies of the POP Movement, we can motivate more educational institutions to adopt sustainable practices, leading to a greener, more sustainable future for all.

Case Studies from Around the World: Schools as Models for Climate Action

Schools are uniquely positioned as learning centers, community hubs, and institutions responsible for shaping future generations. By becoming models for climate action, schools can demonstrate the importance of sustainability and inspire students and the wider community to adopt environmentally friendly practices. This chapter explores how schools can lead climate action through education, infrastructure, community engagement, and policy advocacy.

1. Integrating Climate Education

Curriculum Development: Incorporate climate change and sustainability topics across all subjects. This ensures that every student comprehensively understands environmental issues regardless of their interests or future career path.

Case Study: The Green School in Bali integrates sustainability into every aspect of its curriculum by adopting a hands-on, experiential learning approach that emphasizes real-world applications and environmental stewardship. Students learn about renewable energy through the school's use of solar panels, which is part of its comprehensive renewable energy strategy. This includes a solar PV and microgrid energy management system that significantly reduces the school's carbon footprint (Green School)

(BrightVibes).

In addition to renewable energy, the curriculum covers organic farming and ecological conservation. Students engage in organic farming projects, cultivating their gardens and learning about sustainable agriculture practices. This not only teaches them the importance of organic farming but also provides practical skills in growing food sustainably (Green School).

Ecological conservation is woven into the curriculum through various projects and activities encouraging students to understand and protect their environment. The school's bamboo campus is a testament to its commitment to sustainability, utilizing a rapidly renewable resource and promoting eco-friendly building practices. Moreover, students participate in initiatives such as the BioBus project, which uses biodiesel made from used cooking oil, and other student-driven environmental projects (Green School) (BrightVibes).

This holistic approach ensures that students at the Green School are academically prepared, deeply aware, and committed to sustainable living and environmental conservation.

For more information, please visit the Green School Bali website (Green School).

Professional Development: Provide teachers with the training and resources to teach climate-related topics effectively. Encourage continuous learning and the sharing of best practices.

Example: The National Wildlife Federation offers the Eco-Schools USA program, which equips educators with tools to teach environmental science and sustainability. This program supports schools in creating action teams comprised of students, teachers, administrators, and community volunteers. These teams drive environmental stewardship and education initiatives within their schools. The program provides a flexible framework with various environmental pathways, allowing schools to tailor their approach to meet local needs and goals.

Eco-Schools USA promotes academic benefits and financial savings by encouraging student-led initiatives that improve engagement and understanding of science and significantly reduce energy and water consumption. The program is aligned with national educational standards such as the Next Generation Science Standards (NGSS) and the Common Core State Standards (CCSS), ensuring that environmental education is integrated seamlessly into the existing curriculum.

Through participation in Eco-Schools USA, students gain valuable career readiness skills by leading environmental projects, conducting audits, and developing action plans. This hands-on, experiential learning approach fosters critical thinking, collaboration, and leadership skills, preparing students for future careers in STEM and other fields.

For more detailed information, visit the Eco-Schools USA website (National Wildlife Federation) (The National Wildlife Federation Blog).

2. Sustainable Infrastructure

Green Building Design: Adopt green building standards for new constructions and renovations. This includes using energy-efficient materials, renewable energy sources, and sustainable landscaping.

Example: An excellent example of a green building school in Asia is the Bamboo Sports Hall at Panyaden International School in Thailand. Designed by Chiangmai Life Architects, this sports hall is a remarkable model of sustainable architecture. It accommodates up to 300 students and includes facilities for various sports. Inspired by the lotus flower, the hall integrates seamlessly with the natural landscape and the school's existing earthen and bamboo structures.

The design of the Bamboo Sports Hall ensures a cool and pleasant climate year-round through natural ventilation and insulation, eliminating the need for artificial air conditioning. It features innovative prefabricated bamboo trusses that span over 17 meters without steel reinforcements and is built to withstand high-speed winds and earthquakes. The bamboo used in construction is treated with non-toxic borax salt, contributing to the hall's zero carbon footprint and ensuring a lifespan of at least 50 years. This project demonstrates the effective use of traditional materials in modern construction while highlighting bamboo's environmental and aesthetic benefits.

For more information, please visit the Panyaden International School's Bamboo Sports Hall (BillionBricks) (Eco-Business).

Energy Efficiency: Implement energy-saving measures such as LED lighting, smart thermostats, and energy-efficient appliances. Regular energy audits can help identify further opportunities for savings.

Case Study: The Bronx Design and Construction Academy in New York City successfully reduced its energy consumption by 40% through comprehensive retrofitting and the installation of solar panels. This achievement was part of their commitment to sustainability, which includes initiatives to conserve energy and water, reduce operating costs, and promote a healthy environment for students and staff.

The school collaborated with the Department of Education's Office of Sustainability to implement various energy-saving measures. These measures included upgrading building systems and installing solar panels on the rooftop. The school also engaged in educational activities to raise awareness about environmental responsibility among students.

For more detailed information, you can visit the Bronx Design and Construction Academy's sustainability page (BXDesign) (web).

Water Conservation: Use water-saving fixtures, rainwater harvesting systems, and drought-resistant landscaping to minimize water use.

Example: The University of British Columbia's Center for Interactive Research on Sustainability (CIRS) is a leading example of sustainable building design, featuring advanced systems for rainwater harvesting and greywater recycling. The building collects rainwater, which is then used for potable purposes and irrigation. Additionally, CIRS purifies wastewater through an on-site solar aquatics biofiltration system, effectively recycling greywater for reuse within the building.

This sustainable approach helps the facility meet all its water needs and contributes to its status as a net-positive building in terms of water and energy. By integrating these systems, CIRS reduces its environmental impact, conserves resources, and serves as a model for future sustainable developments.

For more detailed information, you can visit the CIRS page on UBC's website (sustain.ubc.ca) (ArchDaily) (Wikipedia)

3. Community Engagement

Student-Led Initiatives: Encourage students to lead sustainability projects and campaigns. This empowers them to take ownership of climate action and inspires their peers.

Case Study: A notable example of student-led sustainability projects in Europe is the Green Office model at Maastricht University in the Netherlands. The Green Office, established in 2010, serves as a sustainability hub that empowers students and staff to act on sustainability issues. Unlike volunteer-led initiatives, it is supported by the university through funding, a mandate, and office space. This model has been replicated at over 60 universities across Europe, fostering student leadership in sustainability efforts.

Students involved in Green Offices lead various projects, including waste reduction campaigns, energy-saving initiatives, and sustainability education programs. For example, the Green Office at Maastricht University has implemented initiatives like the "Bring Your Own" campaign to reduce single-use plastics and a sustainable food project to promote plant-based diets on campus.

These projects not only help reduce the universities' environmental footprint but also provide students with practical experience in sustainability leadership and project management. The Green Office model has been recognized with the UNESCO-Japan Prize on Education for Sustainable Development for its innovative approach to engaging students in sustainability.

For more detailed information, you can visit the Green Office Movement website (Green Office Movement) (Top Universities).

Another case is at the University of Edinburgh, where the Student Leadership for Sustainability program offers support and extracurricular learning experiences to empower students to take action on sustainability challenges. This program is developed in collaboration with the Students' Association and includes workshops, training sessions, and project opportunities aimed at addressing the climate crisis and promoting sustainable development.

For more information on this program, visit the University of Edinburgh's sustainability page (Times Higher Education (THE)).

Finally, students at Medford High School in Massachusetts successfully launched a campaign to ban plastic straws and bottles from their school. This initiative was driven by a group of environmentally conscious students who recognized the significant environmental impact of single-use plastics. They advocated for reducing plastic waste by implementing a school-wide ban on plastic straws and bottles.

The campaign involved raising awareness about the environmental hazards of plastic pollution, organizing events to educate their peers, and collaborating with school administration to enact the ban. The students' efforts were part of a broader movement to promote sustainability and environmental responsibility within the school community.

For more information, visit the Medford High School website (Wikipedia) (Home - Medford High School).

Partnerships with Local Organizations: Collaborate with local environmental groups, businesses, and government agencies to amplify the impact of school sustainability efforts.

Example: The collaboration between schools and the local government in San Francisco has resulted in comprehensive recycling and composting programs that serve as a model for other cities. San Francisco's Mandatory Recycling and Composting Ordinance, passed in 2009, requires all residents and businesses to separate recyclables, compostables, and trash. This ordinance has significantly contributed to the city's goal of achieving zero waste by 2020 (US EPA) (San Francisco Public Press).

Recology, the city's primary waste management company, plays a crucial role in this initiative. It offers educational programs and tours for schools, teaching students about proper waste sorting and the importance of recycling and composting. These programs help students understand the impact of their actions on the environment and encourage them to participate actively in waste reduction efforts (Recology) (SF Environment).

The city's efforts have led to impressive results, with over 80% of waste being diverted from landfills through recycling and composting. This success is due to strong political leadership, comprehensive education and outreach efforts, and a collaborative approach involving city departments, schools, businesses, and residents (US EPA) (CJIA).

For more information, you can visit the San Francisco Environment Department's website and Recology's educational programs page (Recology) (SF Environment).

Public Awareness Campaigns: Use school events, social media, and local media to raise awareness about climate issues and promote sustainable practices within the community.

Case Study: The "Green Apple Day of Service" organized by the Center for Green Schools at the U.S. Green Building Council engages thousands of students, parents, and community members in sustainability projects worldwide. This initiative began in 2012 and has since mobilized over a million volunteers across 80 countries to participate in activities that promote environmental stewardship and improve learning environments.

Projects carried out during the Green Apple Day of Service range from schoolyard cleanups and garden installations to energy audits and recycling programs. These efforts are designed to advance the three pillars of a green school: environmental impact, health and wellness, and environmental and sustainability literacy. The initiative fosters a sense of collective responsibility and empowers students to lead in sustainability efforts by involving entire school communities.

The Center for Green Schools provides extensive resources to help schools plan and execute their projects. These include project ideas, planning guides, and promotional materials. Schools can register their projects on the Green Apple Day of Service website, which also offers support through funding and volunteer assistance.

For more information, you can visit the official Green Apple Day of Service website (Green Apple) (Green Apple) (Green Apple).

4. Policy Advocacy

School Policies: Develop and enforce school policies that promote sustainability, such as waste reduction, energy conservation, and green procurement.

Example: The Los Angeles Unified School District (LAUSD) has implemented a comprehensive sustainability plan focusing on energy efficiency, waste reduction, and sustainable food sourcing. This initiative aims to make LAUSD one of the most sustainable urban school districts in the United States.

1. **Energy Efficiency**: LAUSD has committed to reducing energy consumption by 20% from its 2014 baseline by 2024. They have implemented several energy-saving measures, including LED lighting retrofits, HVAC upgrades, and energy management systems across many of their campuses. Additionally, the district plans to transition to 100% clean, renewable energy for its electricity needs by 2030 and for all other energy uses by 2040 (Los Angeles Better Buildings Challenge) (The Climate Reality Project).
2. **Waste Reduction**: The district has initiated various waste reduction programs, including comprehensive recycling and composting efforts. These initiatives are part of a broader strategy to minimize waste and promote sustainable practices among students and staff. LAUSD's efforts also include educating the school community about waste reduction through programs and contests such as the "Heros for Zero" contest, which encourages students to engage in activities that contribute to achieving zero net energy readiness (Los Angeles Better Buildings Challenge) (LAUSD).
3. **Sustainable Food Sourcing**: LAUSD is committed to sourcing sustainable food for its school meals. This includes efforts to provide

healthy, locally sourced food options, reducing the environmental impact of food production and transportation. The district has also implemented programs to increase the availability of organic and sustainably produced foods in school cafeterias, contributing to students' overall health and well-being (LAUSD).

For more detailed information, you can visit the LAUSD Sustainability Initiatives Site (LAUSD) and the Climate Reality Project's page on LAUSD's commitment (The Climate Reality Project).

Advocacy for Local and National Policies: Encourage students and staff to advocate for local, state, and national environmental policies. Schools can serve as influential voices in the push for broader systemic change.

Case Study: The "Fridays for Future" movement, inspired by Greta Thunberg, has seen students worldwide join in climate strikes to demand action from policymakers. The movement began in August 2018 when Greta Thunberg, then a 15-year-old student, started striking outside the Swedish Parliament every Friday to protest the lack of action on the climate crisis. Her solitary protest quickly gained international attention, forming a global youth-led movement under the hashtag #FridaysForFuture (Fridays For Future) (Fridays For Future).

Students from various countries have participated in these strikes, including major actions in Europe, the United States, Canada, Australia, and Japan. The movement emphasizes the urgency of the climate crisis and demands that policymakers take immediate and significant actions to limit global warming in line with the Paris Agreement. This includes reducing greenhouse gas emissions and transitioning to renewable energy sources (Clean Energy Wire).

Fridays for Future organizes global strike events, where students skip classes on Fridays to protest and raise awareness about climate change. The movement aims to put moral pressure on political leaders to act on climate science and implement policies that will mitigate the worst effects of global warming (Fridays For Future US).

For more information, please visit the official Fridays for Future website (Fridays For Future) and the Fridays for Future US website (Fridays For Future US).

Another noteworthy example is the POP (Protect Our Planet) Movement, a global youth-led initiative that mobilizes global climate action among young people worldwide. Founded on Earth Day in 2016, the POP Movement aims to empower youth to address climate change through education, capacity building, and action-oriented projects.

One of the central events of the POP Movement is the annual International Conference and POP Festival for Youth-Led Climate Action. This event brings together youth from around the world to share innovative solutions and strategies to combat climate change and advocate for policy change. The POP Festival provides a platform for young leaders to present their projects, engage with global experts, and receive mentorship and support to amplify their impact. The festival emphasizes themes such as climate and health, the role of technology in climate action, and the importance of equity and justice in addressing climate risks (POP Movement).

The POP Movement is active in over 129 countries and collaborates with more than 430 partners, reaching over 2.35 million young people. Through initiatives like tree planting, climate leadership conversations, and regional dialogues, the POP Movement fosters a sense of global solidarity among youth, encouraging them to take collective action to protect the planet and advocate for policy change (POP Movement).

For more information on the POP Movement and its activities, please visit their official website (POP Movement).

Sustainability Reporting: Regularly report on the school's sustainability initiatives and their impact. Transparency builds trust and accountability, encouraging continuous improvement.

Example: The University of California (UC) system publishes an annual sustainability report detailing its progress toward climate action goals and other sustainability initiatives. The report covers various aspects of sustainable operations, including energy efficiency, waste reduction, sustainable food procurement, and reductions in greenhouse gas emissions.

Highlights from the latest 2023 report include UC's commitment to achieving climate neutrality by 2025 for direct emissions (scope 1 and 2) and by 2050 for indirect emissions (scope 3). The report also showcases UC's leadership in renewable energy, with the university entering into its first wind energy contract and achieving significant cost savings through energy efficiency measures. Additionally, the report highlights the integration of anti-racism, diversity, equity, and inclusion principles into their sustainability policies.

The annual sustainability report is a comprehensive document that tracks UC's progress and sets the direction for future initiatives. It is developed with contributions from sustainability offices across all UC campuses, health centers, and affiliated institutions, ensuring a collaborative approach to sustainability.

For more detailed information and to read the full reports, please visit the UC Sustainability Report 2023 and the UC Annual Sustainability Report Page (Sustainability Annual Report 2023) (Sustainability Annual Report 2023) (UCOP).

5. Innovative Programs and Projects

Green Labs and Research Centers: Establish on-campus labs and research centers focused on environmental science and sustainability. These can provide hands-on learning opportunities and contribute to the global body of climate research.

Case Study: The Lund University Centre for Sustainability Studies (LUCSUS) in Sweden is a compelling case study of an on-campus research center focused on environmental science and sustainability. LUCSUS is a renowned institution that combines interdisciplinary education with high-impact research to address global sustainability challenges.

Key Features of LUCSUS:

1. **Interdisciplinary Approach**: LUCSUS emphasizes a holistic view of sustainability, integrating both social and natural sciences. This approach equips students with a broad understanding of the complex interactions between ecological and societal systems.
2. **Research and Education**: LUCSUS offers several master's programs, including the Environmental Studies and Sustainability Science (LUMES) program. These programs provide students with hands-on learning opportunities through case studies and real-world projects, fostering strategic planning and sustainable governance skills.
3. **PhD Program**: The PhD program at LUCSUS focuses on developing future researchers with expertise in sustainability science. The program trains candidates in interdisciplinary research methods and engages them in collaborative projects with social movements, civil society, and policymakers.
4. **Global Impact**: LUCSUS has a strong international presence, with students and researchers worldwide. The center collaborates on global projects and contributes significantly to the global body of climate research through publications and partnerships.
5. **Community Engagement**: The center works closely with various stakeholders, including local communities, to implement sustainable solutions and promote environmental awareness. This engagement ensures that the research conducted at LUCSUS has practical and

meaningful impacts.

For more detailed information, you can visit the Lund University Centre for Sustainability Studies (LUCSUS) website and the Environmental Studies and Sustainability Science program page (Home) (Emerald Insight).

Eco-Friendly Extracurricular Activities: Offer clubs and programs focusing on environmental stewardship, such as gardening clubs, recycling teams, and renewable energy groups.

Example: The Green Schools Alliance's Student Climate & Conservation Congress (Sc3) is a premier leadership training program that empowers student environmental leaders with the skills, knowledge, and tools needed to address climate change and natural resource conservation challenges. Held annually at the U.S. Fish and Wildlife Service's National Conservation Training Center (NCTC), Sc3 brings together outstanding student leaders from across the globe to engage in a week-long intensive program.

Key Features of Sc3:

1. **Leadership Training**: Sc3 provides rigorous leadership training through a combination of workshops, seminars, and hands-on activities. Participants, known as Sc3 Fellows, learn from world-renowned experts and engage in discussions on environmental, social, and economic interconnections that impact sustainability.
2. **Hands-On Projects**: The program includes project-based learning, where students develop and present sustainability projects. These projects are designed to be implemented in their home schools and communities, fostering real-world impact and encouraging practical applications of their training.
3. **Community and Networking**: Sc3 creates a unique community of like-minded young environmentalists. Participants form lasting connections with peers, mentors, and experts, creating a support

network that continues beyond the congress.
4. **Expanding Impact**: Sc3 has expanded to include regional summits in addition to the national congress. These summits offer more localized training opportunities, allowing more students to participate and benefit from the program's resources and expertise.

For more information about the Student Climate & Conservation Congress (Sc3) and to explore participation opportunities, you can visit the Green Schools Alliance website (The Green Schools Alliance).

Sustainable Transportation: Promote and facilitate the use of sustainable transportation options such as biking, walking, carpooling, and public transit.

Case Study: Portland Public Schools (PPS) in Oregon, in collaboration with the Portland Bureau of Transportation (PBOT) and other local partners, has implemented a comprehensive Safe Routes to School program. This initiative encourages students to walk, bike, and use other forms of active transportation to get to and from school, significantly reducing carbon emissions from school commutes.

The Safe Routes to School program focuses on improving infrastructure and providing education to ensure safe travel for students. Key elements include:

1. **Infrastructure Improvements**: The program has made significant investments in enhancing street safety around schools. This includes installing better crosswalks, bike lanes, sidewalks, and traffic calming measures. These improvements make it safer and more convenient for students to walk and bike to school (Portland.gov) (Portland.gov).
2. **Educational Campaigns**: PBOT conducts safety education programs that teach students about pedestrian and bicycle safety. These programs are integrated into the school curriculum and include activities like bike rodeos and pedestrian safety drills (Portland.gov).

3. **Community Engagement**: The program actively involves parents, students, and school administrators in identifying the safest routes to school and the barriers that need to be addressed. This community-driven approach ensures that the program meets the specific needs of each school community (Portland.gov).
4. **Sustainability Goals**: By promoting walking and biking, the program not only enhances student health and well-being but also contributes to the city's broader environmental goals by reducing traffic congestion and carbon emissions associated with school commutes (Portland.gov).

For more detailed information about the Safe Routes to School program in Portland and its various initiatives, you can visit the Portland Safe Routes to School page and the PPS Safe Routes to School page (Portland.gov) (PPS).

By implementing these strategies, schools can serve as powerful models for climate action. They can demonstrate the feasibility and benefits of sustainable practices, educate future generations, and inspire broader societal change. As students, teachers, and communities witness the positive impacts of these efforts, the momentum for addressing climate change will continue to grow.

Regenerative Activities for Schools to Tackle Climate Change

Regenerative activities go beyond traditional methods by fostering creativity, innovation, and hands-on learning experiences that empower students to become active participants in addressing climate change. These activities integrate environmental education with real-world applications, making sustainability a dynamic and engaging part of the school culture.

1. **Solar Energy Workshops**

Organize hands-on workshops where students design and build small solar-powered devices such as phone chargers, fans, or miniature cars. These workshops can include lessons on solar panel installation and maintenance.

Benefits: Promotes understanding of renewable energy and practical skills development.

Reference: Solar Energy International

2. **Hydroponic Farming Projects**

Implement hydroponic systems in classrooms or greenhouses to grow vegetables and herbs without soil. Students can learn about water conservation, plant biology, and sustainable agriculture practices.

Benefits: Reduces water usage, teaches sustainable farming techniques, and provides fresh produce.

Reference: Hydroponic Society of America

3. Eco-Innovation Challenges

Host school-wide competitions where students create innovative solutions to environmental problems. Categories can include waste reduction, energy efficiency, or pollution control, with winners receiving awards and the opportunity to implement their projects.

Benefits: Encourages creative thinking, problem-solving skills, and community involvement.

Reference: Ashoka's Youth Venture

4. Green Energy Clubs

Form student clubs dedicated to exploring and promoting green energy technologies. Activities can include building wind turbines, experimenting with biofuels, and creating energy-efficient prototypes.

Benefits: Fosters teamwork, leadership, and a deep understanding of renewable energy sources.

Reference: Green Schools National Network

5. Sustainable Product Design

Incorporate lessons on sustainable product design into art and technology classes. Students can create products from recycled materials or design eco-friendly packaging solutions.

Benefits: Develops design thinking, creativity, and awareness of sustainable practices.

Reference: Cradle to Cradle Products Innovation Institute

6. Climate Change Hackathons

Organize hackathons focused on developing digital solutions to combat climate change. Students can work on apps, websites, or software that promote environmental awareness, track carbon footprints, or optimize resource use.

Benefits: Enhances coding skills, promotes innovation, and addresses real-world issues.

Reference: Code for Climate

7. Community Renewable Energy Projects

Engage students in designing and implementing renewable energy projects for the local community, such as solar-powered streetlights or community gardens with renewable irrigation systems.

Benefits: Provides practical experience, strengthens community ties, and promotes sustainability.

Reference: Community Power Network

8. Eco-Art Installations

Encourage students to create art installations from reclaimed materials that highlight environmental issues. These can be displayed around the school or community to raise awareness and inspire action.

Benefits: Combines art and activism, encourages recycling, and raises environmental awareness.

Reference: Environmental Art

9. Permaculture Design Projects

Introduce students to permaculture principles by designing sustainable, self-sufficient gardens and landscapes. Projects can include food forests, rain gardens, and wildlife habitats.

Benefits: Teaches sustainable agriculture, biodiversity, and ecological design.

Reference: Permaculture Institute

10. Environmental Storytelling

Incorporate environmental themes into storytelling, theater, and media production classes. Students can create documentaries, podcasts, or plays that explore climate change and sustainability.

Benefits: Enhances communication skills, creativity, and environmental awareness.

Reference: Storytelling for Change

11. Energy Monitoring Programs

Set up student-led initiatives to monitor and report on the school's energy usage. Students can use data to suggest improvements and track the impact of energy-saving measures.

Benefits: Provides hands-on experience with data analysis, promotes energy conservation.

Reference: Alliance to Save Energy

12. Eco-Entrepreneurship Programs

Create programs where students develop and pitch eco-friendly business ideas. This can include creating business plans, conducting market research, and presenting to a panel of judges.

Benefits: Fosters entrepreneurship, innovation, and a practical understanding of sustainable business practices.

Reference: Youth Entrepreneurship Programs

13. Citizen Science Projects

Involve students in citizen science projects that contribute to real environmental research. Activities can include monitoring local air and water quality, tracking wildlife populations, or participating in climate data collection.

Benefits: Connects students to scientific research, promotes active learning and community engagement.

Reference: National Geographic's Citizen Science Projects

14. Energy-Efficient Architecture Models

In architecture and engineering classes, have students design models of energy-efficient buildings. This can include exploring passive solar design, green roofs, and sustainable materials.

Benefits: Teaches principles of sustainable architecture, engineering skills, and environmental impact.

Reference: Architecture 2030

15. Environmental Policy Simulation Games

Use simulation games to teach students about environmental policy and decision-making. Students can role-play as government officials, activists, or business leaders to explore the complexities of environmental governance.

Benefits: Enhances understanding of policy-making, critical thinking, and collaborative problem-solving.

Reference: The World Climate Simulation

By engaging in these regenerative activities, schools can foster a culture of innovation and environmental stewardship, empowering students to be leaders in the fight against climate change. These activities provide practical, hands-on experiences that not only educate but also inspire students to take meaningful action in their communities.

99 Ways for Schools to Save Money and the Planet

This comprehensive list is designed to help schools reduce costs and promote environmental responsibility through sustainable practices. A reference for further information and guidance accompanies each practice.

1. **Install Solar Panels**: Not only does this practice reduce electricity costs, but it also generates renewable energy on-site, leading to significant long-term savings. *Reference*: Energy.gov
2. **Use Energy-Efficient Lighting (LED Bulbs)**: Cuts down energy consumption and lasts longer than traditional bulbs. *Reference*: Energy.gov
3. **Implement Motion Sensor Lighting**: Reduces energy use by turning off lights in unoccupied areas. *Reference*: EPA
4. **Utilize Natural Light**: Installing skylights or larger windows reduces the need for artificial lighting. *Reference*: National Renewable Energy Laboratory (NREL)
5. **Install Programmable Thermostats**: Optimizes heating and cooling schedules, reducing energy waste. *Reference*: Energy Star
6. **Upgrade to Energy-Efficient HVAC Systems**: Improves efficiency and lowers energy bills. *Reference*: DOE
7. **Implement a School-Wide Recycling Program**: Reduces waste disposal costs and promotes environmental responsibility. *Reference*: EPA

8. **Start a Composting Program**: Reduces waste and creates nutrient-rich soil for school gardens. *Reference*: NRDC
9. **Use Rainwater Harvesting Systems**: Reduces water costs using collected rainwater for irrigation. *Reference*: EPA
10. **Plant Native and Drought-Resistant Plants**: Lowers water usage and maintenance costs. *Reference*: USDA
11. **Implement Green Roofing Systems**: Improves insulation and reduces heating/cooling costs. *Reference*: EPA
12. **Encourage Carpooling or Biking to School**: Reduces transportation costs and carbon footprint. *Reference*: Safe Routes to School
13. **Transition to a Digital Curriculum**: Saves on paper, printing, and textbook costs. *Reference*: EdTech Magazine
14. **Install Water-Saving Fixtures in Bathrooms**: Lowers water usage and utility bills. *Reference*: EPA WaterSense
15. **Use Solar Water Heaters**: Reduces water heating costs using renewable energy. *Reference*: Energy.gov
16. **Conduct Regular Maintenance on School Buses**: Improves fuel efficiency and reduces emissions. *Reference*: National Association for Pupil Transportation (NAPT)
17. **Invest in Electric or Hybrid School Buses**: Reduces fuel costs and emissions. *Reference*: EPA
18. **Install Bike Racks**: Encourages cycling, reducing car traffic and parking needs. *Reference*: League of American Bicyclists
19. **Set Up an Energy Audit**: Identifies areas for energy efficiency improvements. *Reference*: Energy Star
20. **Use Eco-Friendly Cleaning Products**: Often cheaper in bulk and safer for the environment. *Reference*: EPA
21. **Implement a Paperless Communication System**: Saves on paper and printing costs. *Reference*: Edutopia
22. **Use Recycled Paper for Printing**: Reduces costs and environmental impact. *Reference*: NRDC
23. **Host Environmental Education Programs**: Raise awareness and drive school-wide action. *Reference*: National Environmental Education

Foundation (NEEF)
24. **Organize Tree Planting Events**: Improves air quality and provides shade, reducing cooling costs. *Reference*: Arbor Day Foundation
25. **Partner with Local Farms for Farm-to-School Programs**: Reduces food transportation costs and supports local agriculture. *Reference*: National Farm to School Network
26. **Create a Student-Run Garden**: Provides fresh produce for the cafeteria and hands-on learning. *Reference*: KidsGardening.org
27. **Encourage Students to Bring Reusable Water Bottles**: Reduce plastic waste and disposable cups/bottles costs. *Reference*: EPA
28. **Install Water Bottle Refilling Stations**: Encourages reusable bottles and reduces waste. *Reference*: Healthy Schools Campaign
29. **Reduce Cafeteria Food Waste**: Better meal planning minimizes waste and costs. *Reference*: NRDC
30. **Donate Excess Food to Local Shelters**: Reduces waste and helps the community. *Reference*: Feeding America
31. **Use Energy-Efficient Kitchen Appliances**: Lowers energy consumption and utility bills. *Reference*: Energy Star
32. **Conduct Regular Energy Usage Assessments**: Identifies waste and areas for improvement. *Reference*: Energy Star
33. **Insulate Buildings**: Reduces heating and cooling costs by improving energy efficiency. *Reference*: Energy.gov
34. **Replace Old Windows with Energy-Efficient Ones**: Improves insulation and reduces energy bills. *Reference*: Energy Star
35. **Implement a "Green Team" of Students and Staff**: Oversees sustainability initiatives and ensures accountability. *Reference*: Green Schools National Network
36. **Create a Sustainability Curriculum**: This practice not only educates students on environmental stewardship but also empowers them to take practical actions, fostering a sense of responsibility and inspiring future generations. *Reference*: USGBC Center for Green Schools
37. **Partner with Local Businesses for Sustainability Projects**: Leverages resources and support from the community. *Reference*: EPA

38. **Install Charging Stations for Electric Vehicles**: Encourages the use of electric cars and reduces emissions. *Reference*: DOE
39. **Encourage a No-Idling Policy for Cars and Buses**: Reduces fuel consumption and emissions. *Reference*: EPA
40. **Use Online Textbooks and Resources**: Saves money on physical textbooks and reduces paper use. *Reference*: EdTech Magazine
41. **Offer Incentives for Students Who Practice Sustainable Habits**: Encourages behavior that benefits the environment. *Reference*: Green Schools Alliance
42. **Promote a "Reduce, Reuse, Recycle" Culture**: Minimizes waste and promotes sustainability. *Reference*: EPA
43. **Install Ceiling Fans**: Reduces the need for air conditioning. *Reference*: Energy.gov
44. **Use Eco-Friendly Landscaping Practices**: Saves water and reduces maintenance costs. *Reference*: USDA
45. **Conduct Energy-Saving Competitions Among Classes**: Encourages energy conservation through friendly competition. *Reference*: Green Schools Alliance
46. **Use Sustainable Materials for School Construction and Renovations**: Reduces environmental impact and can lower costs in the long term. *Reference*: USGBC
47. **Switch to Eco-Friendly School Uniforms**: Promotes sustainability and can reduce costs with durable, long-lasting materials. *Reference*: Sustainable Apparel Coalition
48. **Offer Training for Staff on Energy Conservation**: Educate staff on best practices for reducing energy use. *Reference*: Energy Star
49. **Implement a Sustainable Procurement Policy**: Ensures that purchased products and services are environmentally friendly. *Reference*: EPA
50. **Use Reclaimed or Recycled Materials for Art Projects**: Saves money and promotes creativity with sustainable materials. *Reference*: National Art Education Association
51. **Organize Eco-Friendly Fundraising Events**: Reduces waste and

promotes sustainability. *Reference*: Green Schools National Network

52. **Promote a "Lights Out" Policy in Unused Rooms**: Saves energy by turning off lights in unoccupied spaces. *Reference*: Energy Star
53. **Use Double-Sided Printing**: Saves paper and reduces costs. *Reference*: NRDC
54. **Encourage Digital Note-Taking**: Reduces paper use and promotes tech skills. *Reference*: Edutopia
55. **Implement a Bike-to-School Program with Incentives**: Promotes healthy, sustainable transportation. *Reference*: Safe Routes to School
56. **Utilize Cloud Storage**: Reduces the need for physical servers and saves energy. *Reference*: Energy Star
57. **Create a Lending Library for School Supplies**: Reduces the need for new purchases and promotes sharing. *Reference*: Edutopia
58. **Install Wind Turbines**: Generating renewable energy on-site reduces electricity costs. *Reference*: DOE
59. **Start a Battery Recycling Program**: Reduces waste and promotes sustainability. *According to the EPA, this is a simple yet effective way to reduce the school's environmental impact. For more information on how to start a battery recycling program, please refer to [US EPA].*
60. **Offer a Reusable Lunch Container Program**: Reduces waste from disposable containers. *Reference*: Eco-Schools USA
61. **Use Second-Hand Furniture and Equipment**: Saves money and reduces waste. *Reference*: Sustainable Schools Project
62. **Grow a School Vegetable Garden**: Supplements the cafeteria with fresh produce and educate students. *Reference*: KidsGardening.org
63. **Introduce a Zero-Waste Policy**: Minimizes waste and promotes sustainability. *Reference*: Zero Waste International Alliance
64. **Optimize Transportation Routes for Efficiency**: Saves fuel and reduces emissions. *Reference*: National Association for Pupil Transportation (NAPT)
65. **Host Clothing and Book Swaps Among Students**: Reduces waste and promotes reuse. *Reference*: Green Schools Alliance
66. **Organize Community Clean-Up Events**: Promotes environmental

stewardship and can beautify the school. *Reference*: Keep America Beautiful

67. **Use Energy-Efficient Outdoor Lighting**: Reduces energy consumption and costs. *Reference*: Energy Star
68. **Promote Vegetarian or Plant-Based Meal Options**: Reduces school meals' carbon footprint. *Reference*: School Nutrition Association
69. **Use Recycled or Bamboo-Based Paper Products**: Saves trees and reduces environmental impact. *Reference*: NRDC
70. **Install Low-Flow Toilets and Faucets**: Reduces water usage and utility bills. *Reference*: EPA WaterSense
71. **Use Eco-Friendly Paint and Materials for Renovations**: Reduces harmful emissions and can be cost-effective. *Reference*: EPA
72. **Encourage Students to Participate in Local Environmental Projects**: Promotes community involvement and environmental responsibility. *Reference*: NEEF
73. **Implement a Rain Garden to Manage Stormwater**: Reduces flooding and promotes biodiversity. *Reference*: EPA
74. **Use Digital Signage Instead of Printed Posters**: Saves paper and reduces waste. *Reference*: Energy Star
75. **Incorporate Sustainability into School Events and Projects**: Promotes awareness and action. *Reference*: Green Schools Alliance
76. **Provide Professional Development on Climate Education**: Equips teachers with the knowledge to educate students on climate action. *Reference*: USGBC Center for Green Schools
77. **Offer Incentives for Staff to Reduce Their Carbon Footprint**: Encourages sustainable behaviors among staff. *Reference*: Green Schools National Network
78. **Encourage Reusable Shopping Bags in the School Store**: Reduces plastic waste and promotes sustainability. *Reference*: NRDC
79. **Set Up a "Take Only What You Need" Policy in the Cafeteria**: Reduces food waste and costs. *Reference*: NRDC
80. **Conduct Regular Waste Audits**: Identifies areas for improvement and reduces waste. *Reference*: EPA

81. **Use Biogas for Cooking in the Cafeteria Where Feasible**: Reduces energy costs and uses renewable resources. *Reference*: EPA
82. **Partner with Environmental Organizations for Resources and Support**: Leverages expertise and resources. *Reference*: NEEF
83. **Implement Energy-Efficient Computer Settings (Sleep Mode)**: Saves energy and reduces costs. *Reference*: Energy Star
84. **Use Green Building Standards for New Constructions**: Ensures sustainable and cost-effective buildings. *Reference*: USGBC
85. **Replace Single-Use Items with Reusable Alternatives**: Reduces waste and long-term costs. *Reference*: Zero Waste International Alliance
86. **Install Energy-Efficient Exit Signs**: Lowers energy consumption and maintenance costs. *Reference*: Energy Star
87. **Promote a "Walk to School" Day**: Encourages healthy, sustainable transportation. *Reference*: Safe Routes to School
88. **Create a Rainwater Garden for Educational Purposes**: Teaches students about water conservation and biodiversity. *Reference*: EPA
89. **Use Smart Power Strips to Reduce Phantom Energy Use**: Saves energy and reduces costs. *Reference*: Energy Star
90. **Encourage using Digital Homework Submissions**: Saves paper and promotes tech skills. *Reference*: Edutopia
91. **Install Reflective Window Film to Reduce Heat Gain**: Improves insulation and reduces cooling costs. *Reference*: Energy.gov
92. **Use Local and Seasonal Produce in the Cafeteria**: Reduces transportation costs and supports local agriculture. *Reference*: National Farm to School Network
93. **Set Up a School Swap Shop for Uniforms and Supplies**: Reduces waste and promotes reuse. *Reference*: Green Schools Alliance
94. **Develop a Carpooling App for Parents and Students**: Encourages carpooling and reduces transportation costs. *Reference*: Safe Routes to School
95. **Conduct Environmental Impact Assessments for School Activities**: Identifies areas for improvement and promotes sustainability. *Reference*: EPA

96. **Encourage Teachers to Integrate Sustainability into Their Lessons**: Promotes awareness and action among students. *Reference*: USGBC Center for Green Schools
97. **Host Workshops on Energy Conservation at Home**: Educates the school community on saving energy and money. *Reference*: Energy Star
98. **Use Solar Outdoor Lighting**: Reduces energy costs and utilizes renewable energy. *Reference*: DOE
99. **Celebrate Earth Day with School-Wide Events and Activities**: Raises awareness and encourages sustainable practices. - *Reference*: Earth Day Network

If you have found this book helpful, so far, we would appreciate it if you left us a favorable review!

Sustainable Schools Can Save

Here is a detailed list of how much money schools can save in dollar terms by implementing various sustainability initiatives, along with potential costs if these actions are not taken:

1. **Embracing Renewable Energy**

   - **Savings**: Schools can save between $10,000 and $20,000 annually by installing solar panels, depending on their size and energy consumption (Lets Go Zero) (Schools Week).
   - **Costs if Not Undertaken**: Schools could face increasing electricity costs without adopting renewable energy, potentially paying $15,000 to $25,000 more per year due to rising fossil fuel prices (Take Action Global).

2. **Enhancing Energy Efficiency**

   - **Savings**: Retrofitting with LED lighting and better insulation can save $5,000 to $10,000 per year on electricity bills and up to $15,000 on heating and cooling costs (Lets Go Zero) (Schools Week).
   - **Costs if Not Undertaken**: Using inefficient energy could lead to an extra $10,000 to $20,000 per year in energy bills (Take Action Global).

3. Water Conservation

- **Savings**: Installing low-flow fixtures and fixing leaks can save schools $2,000 to $5,000 annually (Take Action Global).
- **Costs if Not Undertaken**: Not addressing water waste could result in paying $3,000 to $6,000 more yearly due to rising water costs and penalties for excessive use (Take Action Global).

4. Waste Reduction and Recycling

- **Savings**: Effective recycling programs can save $1,000 to $2,000 annually in disposal costs (Lets Go Zero).
- **Costs if Not Undertaken**: Without recycling, schools may incur $1,500 to $3,000 more in waste management fees (Lets Go Zero).

5. Green Transportation Initiatives

- **Savings**: Encouraging biking and walking can save $1,000 to $3,000 annually by reducing bus service costs (Lets Go Zero).
- **Costs if Not Undertaken**: Relying on traditional transportation methods could increase costs by $2,000 to $4,000 per year due to fuel price hikes and maintenance (Lets Go Zero).

6. Implementing Sustainable Curriculum and Community Involvement

- **Savings**: These programs often have indirect financial benefits such as grants and reduced operational costs, potentially saving $1,000 to $5,000 per year (Take Action Global).
- **Costs if Not Undertaken**: Lack of involvement can lead to missed opportunities for grants and community support, resulting in higher operational costs by $2,000 to $5,000 annually (Take Action Global).

7. Adopting Sustainable Food Practices

- **Savings**: Reducing food waste and promoting plant-based diets can save $500 to $1,000 annually (Lets Go Zero).
- **Costs if Not Undertaken**: Food waste can cost schools an additional $500 to $1,000 per year (Lets Go Zero).

8. Conducting Eco-Friendly School Events

- **Savings**: Hosting green events can save $500 to $1,000 annually on materials and waste management (Take Action Global).
- **Costs if Not Undertaken**: Traditional events can incur $1,000 to $2,000 more per year due to higher material and disposal costs (Take Action Global).

9. Long-Term Investments in Sustainability

- **Savings**: Investing in long-term sustainability can save schools $10,000 to $30,000 annually through various cost-cutting measures (Schools Week).
- **Costs if Not Undertaken**: Failure to invest can result in $15,000 to $35,000 in additional annual costs due to inefficiencies and rising energy prices (Schools Week).

10. Embracing a Sustainable Future for Schools

- **Savings**: Comprehensive sustainability plans can save schools up to $50,000 annually through combined energy, water, and waste management savings (Take Action Global).
- **Costs if Not Undertaken**: Without a sustainable approach, schools could face $60,000 to $80,000 in additional costs per year due to inefficiencies and rising utility prices (Take Action Global).

11. Undertaking Regenerative Activities for Schools to Tackle Climate Change

- **Savings**: Engaging in regenerative activities can save $5,000 to $15,000 annually through improved ecosystem services and resource management (Take Action Global).
- **Costs if Not Undertaken**: Ignoring regenerative practices could lead to $7,000 to $20,000 in additional costs per year due to environmental degradation and resource depletion (Take Action Global).

References

- Let's Go Zero Campaign (Lets Go Zero)
- Take Action Global (Take Action Global)
- Schools Week Analysis (Schools Week)
- Transform Our World (Transform Our World)

These actions allow schools to realize substantial financial benefits while contributing to a sustainable future. The costs of inaction, on the other hand, can lead to significantly higher expenses and missed opportunities for savings.

Costs of Inaction

A 1-degree Celsius (1.8-degree Fahrenheit) increase in global temperature leads to a 12 percent decline in world gross domestic product (GDP). Research has found that this level of economic damage wrought by climate change is six times worse than previously thought, with global warming set to shrink wealth at a rate consistent with the financial losses of a continuing permanent war (Nature).

Here is a detailed list of economic, absenteeism, and health costs of inaction with explanations and references:

Economic Costs

1.Increased Energy Costs:

- **Explanation**: Without implementing renewable energy sources such as solar panels or wind turbines, schools will continue to face rising energy bills due to increasing electricity prices and reliance on fossil fuels.
- **Cost**: Schools may spend an additional $10,000 to $25,000 annually on energy bills (World Resources Institute) (Lets Go Zero).
- **Reference**: Let's Go Zero Campaign (Lets Go Zero); World Resources Institute (World Resources Institute).

2. Higher Maintenance and Operational Costs:

- **Explanation**: Due to inefficient systems, schools that do not invest in energy-efficient infrastructure (e.g., LED lighting, insulation) will have higher ongoing maintenance and operational costs.
- **Cost**: Potentially $5,000 to $15,000 more annually in energy expenses (Lets Go Zero) (Schools Week).
- **Reference**: Schools Week (Schools Week).

3. Waste Management Costs:

- **Explanation**: Schools that do not implement waste reduction and recycling programs will incur higher waste disposal costs.
- **Cost**: An additional $500 to $2,000 annually (Lets Go Zero).
- **Reference**: Let's Go Zero Campaign (Lets Go Zero).

4. Transportation Costs:

- **Explanation**: Without promoting green transportation options (e.g., biking, walking), schools will continue to bear higher transportation costs due to increased bus service usage and fuel prices.
- **Cost**: Potentially $1,000 to $3,000 more annually (World Resources Institute) (Lets Go Zero).
- **Reference**: World Resources Institute (World Resources Institute); Let's Go Zero Campaign (Lets Go Zero).

5. Long-Term Infrastructure Costs:

- **Explanation**: Neglecting investments in sustainable infrastructure can result in higher long-term maintenance and operational costs.
- **Cost**: Potentially $10,000 to $20,000 more annually (Schools Week).
- **Reference**: Schools Week (Schools Week).

Absenteeism Costs

1. Increased Absenteeism Due to Poor Air Quality:

- **Explanation**: Schools that do not reduce reliance on fossil fuels and improve air quality may experience higher absenteeism rates due to respiratory illnesses among students and staff.
- **Cost**: Approximately $1,000 to $2,000 annually per school in lost funding and increased healthcare costs due to higher absenteeism (World Resources Institute) (Yale Climate Connections).
- **Reference**: Yale Climate Connections (Yale Climate Connections).

2. Health-Related Absenteeism:

- **Explanation**: Poor indoor air quality and insufficient heating or cooling systems can lead to increased illness-related absenteeism.
- **Cost**: Potentially $500 to $1,000 annually per 100 students due to illness-related absences (World Resources Institute) (Lets Go Zero).
- **Reference**: World Resources Institute (World Resources Institute); Let's Go Zero Campaign (Lets Go Zero).

Health Costs

1. Increased Healthcare Costs:

- **Explanation**: Poor air quality and lack of green spaces can lead to higher rates of asthma, respiratory conditions, and other health issues, increasing healthcare costs.
- **Cost**: $1,000 to $3,000 annually per school (World Resources Institute) (Yale Climate Connections).
- **Reference**: World Resources Institute (World Resources Institute); Yale Climate Connections (Yale Climate Connections).

2. Unhealthy Diets:

- **Explanation**: Schools that do not adopt sustainable food practices and continue offering high meat-based diets can contribute to higher rates of obesity and related diseases, increasing healthcare costs.
- **Cost**: $500 to $1,000 annually per school (World Resources Institute).
- **Reference**: World Resources Institute (World Resources Institute).

3. Mental Health Costs:

- **Explanation**: Lack of green spaces and outdoor activities can negatively impact students' mental health, leading to increased spending on mental health services.
- **Cost**: $1,000 to $2,000 annually per school (Lets Go Zero).
- **Reference**: Let's Go Zero Campaign (Lets Go Zero).

References:

- **Let's Go Zero Campaign**: Provides practical ideas and examples for schools to reduce their carbon footprint and save money (Lets Go Zero).
- **World Resources Institute**: Discusses the economic benefits and costs associated with clean energy investments and sustainability measures (World Resources Institute).
- **Yale Climate Connections**: Offers insights into the health and economic impacts of climate action and inaction (Yale Climate Connections).
- **Schools Week**: Analyzes the costs and challenges schools face in implementing sustainability initiatives (Schools Week).

Implementing sustainable practices contributes to environmental health, offers significant financial savings, and reduces absenteeism and healthcare costs.

Key Terms and Definitions

This section outlines some useful key terms and definitions.

Carbon Footprint

- **Definition**: The total amount of greenhouse gases (GHGs) emitted directly and indirectly by human activities, measured in units of carbon dioxide equivalents.
- **Reference**: EPA, Carbon Footprint

Energy Efficiency

- **Definition**: Using less energy to perform the same task or produce the same outcome reduces energy waste.
- **Reference**: U.S. Department of Energy, Energy Efficiency

Renewable Energy

- **Definition**: Energy from sources that are naturally replenishing but flow-limited, such as solar, wind, and hydropower.
- **Reference**: National Renewable Energy Laboratory (NREL), Renewable Energy

Sustainability

- **Definition**: Meeting the needs of the present without compromising the ability of future generations to meet their own needs, encompassing environmental, social, and economic dimensions.
- **Reference**: Brundtland Report, Our Common Future

Green Building

- **Definition**: The practice of designing, constructing, and operating buildings to minimize environmental impact, enhance occupant health, and reduce energy consumption.
- **Reference**: U.S. Green Building Council (USGBC), Green Building

Waste Diversion

- **Definition**: The process of redirecting waste from landfills through recycling, composting, and other methods.
- **Reference**: EPA, Waste Diversion

Sustainable Procurement

- **Definition**: The process of purchasing goods and services that have a reduced impact on the environment and society throughout their lifecycle.
- **Reference**: United Nations Environment Programme (UNEP), Sustainable Procurement

Water Conservation

- **Definition**: Practices and technologies designed to reduce water use and waste, ensuring the availability of water for future generations.
- **Reference**: EPA, Water Conservation

Biodiversity

- **Definition**: The variety of all forms of life on Earth, including different species, ecosystems, and genetic variations.
- **Reference**: Convention on Biological Diversity, Biodiversity

Climate Change

- **Definition**: Long-term changes in temperature, precipitation, and other atmospheric conditions on Earth, largely driven by human activities such as burning fossil fuels.
- **Reference**: Intergovernmental Panel on Climate Change (IPCC), Climate Change

Ecosystem Services

- **Definition**: The benefits people obtain from ecosystems, including provisioning, regulating, cultural, and supporting services.
- **Reference**: Millennium Ecosystem Assessment, Ecosystem Services

Environmental Justice

- **Definition**: The fair treatment and meaningful involvement of all people, regardless of race, color, national origin, or income, with respect to the development, implementation, and enforcement of environmental laws, regulations, and policies.
- **Reference**: EPA, Environmental Justice

Net Zero Energy Building

- **Definition**: A building that produces as much energy as it consumes over the course of a year, typically through energy efficiency and renewable energy generation.

KEY TERMS AND DEFINITIONS

- **Reference**: U.S. Department of Energy, Net Zero Energy

Greenhouse Gas (GHG)

- **Definition**: Gases that trap heat in the atmosphere, contributing to the greenhouse effect and climate change. Examples include carbon dioxide, methane, and nitrous oxide.
- **Reference**: EPA, Greenhouse Gases

Circular Economy

- **Definition**: An economic system aimed at eliminating waste and the continual use of resources through recycling, reusing, and refurbishing materials.
- **Reference**: Ellen MacArthur Foundation, Circular Economy

Sustainable Development Goals (SDGs)

- **Definition**: A collection of 17 global goals set by the United Nations General Assembly to address global challenges and achieve a better and more sustainable future by 2030.
- **Reference**: United Nations, Sustainable Development Goals

Energy Audit

- **Definition**: An assessment that evaluates how energy is used in a building and identifies opportunities for energy savings.
- **Reference**: U.S. Department of Energy, Energy Audit

Lifecycle Assessment (LCA)

- **Definition**: A technique to assess the environmental impacts associated with all stages of a product's life, from raw material extraction through

to disposal.
- **Reference**: EPA, Lifecycle Assessment

Environmental Impact Assessment (EIA)

- **Definition**: A process of evaluating the potential environmental effects of a proposed project or development.
- **Reference**: International Association for Impact Assessment, Environmental Impact Assessment

Sustainable Agriculture

- **Definition**: Farming practices that meet current food needs without compromising the ability of future generations to meet their needs, emphasizing environmental health, economic profitability, and social equity.
- **Reference**: Food and Agriculture Organization (FAO), Sustainable Agriculture

These key terms and definitions provide a foundational understanding of the concepts discussed in the book and serve as a valuable reference for readers seeking to deepen their knowledge of sustainability in schools and beyond.

Resources for Educators

1. Energy Efficiency and Renewable Energy

U.S. Department of Energy (DOE) - Energy Efficiency and Renewable Energy (EERE)

- Website: energy.gov/eere
- Resources: Guides on energy efficiency, renewable energy technologies, and grants available for schools.

ENERGY STAR for K-12 School Districts

- Website: energystar.gov
- Resources: Tools and resources for energy benchmarking, improvement projects, and recognition programs.

2. Waste Reduction and Recycling

Environmental Protection Agency (EPA) - WasteWise Program

- Website: epa.gov/smm/wastewise
- Resources: Information on waste reduction, recycling, and reusing materials, as well as case studies and tools for schools.

Keep America Beautiful

- Website: kab.org
- Resources: Programs and resources for recycling, litter prevention, and beautification, including the Great American Cleanup.

3. Sustainable Transportation

Safe Routes to School National Partnership

- Website: saferoutespartnership.org
- Resources: Strategies and resources to promote walking and biking to school, improving safety and reducing traffic.

U.S. Department of Transportation (DOT) - Federal Transit Administration

- Website: transit.dot.gov
- Resources: Information on public transit options and grants to support school transportation initiatives.

4. Green Spaces and Outdoor Learning

National Wildlife Federation (NWF) - Schoolyard Habitats®

- Website: nwf.org
- Resources: Guidance on creating and certifying schoolyard habitats, lesson plans, and educational resources.

American Society of Landscape Architects (ASLA)

- Website: asla.org
- Resources: Ideas and case studies for creating sustainable school

landscapes and outdoor learning environments.

5. Water Conservation

EPA WaterSense for Schools

- Website: epa.gov/watersense
- Resources: Tools and resources for water conservation, including best practices for reducing water use in schools.

Alliance for Water Efficiency (AWE)

- Website: allianceforwaterefficiency.org
- Resources: Information on water efficiency practices, programs, and technologies suitable for schools.

6. Sustainable Food Practices

National Farm to School Network

- Website: farmtoschool.org
- Resources: Guides, toolkits, and case studies on implementing farm-to-school programs, promoting local food, and improving nutrition.

USDA - Farm to School Program

- Website: fns.usda.gov
- Resources: Grants, training, and resources to support farm-to-school activities and connect schools with local farmers.

7. Eco-Friendly School Events

Green Sports Alliance

- Website: greensportsalliance.org
- Resources: Strategies and tools for greening school sports events and other large gatherings.

Natural Resources Defense Council (NRDC) - Greening Your Celebrations

- Website: nrdc.org
- Resources: Tips and resources for hosting eco-friendly events and celebrations.

8. Long-Term Sustainability Investments

U.S. Green Building Council (USGBC) - LEED Certification

- Website: usgbc.org
- Resources: Information on LEED certification for schools, green building standards, and case studies.

Environmental Protection Agency (EPA) - Environmentally Preferable Purchasing (EPP)

- Website: epa.gov/greenerproducts
- Resources: Guidance on sustainable procurement policies and choosing environmentally preferable products.

9. Federal Emergency Management Agency (FEMA) - Building Resilience

- Website: fema.gov
- Resources: Information on building resilience to extreme weather events and emergency preparedness for schools.

10. Additional Educational Resources

National Environmental Education Foundation (NEEF)

- Website: neefusa.org
- Resources: Environmental education resources, grants, and tools to integrate sustainability into the curriculum.

Project Learning Tree (PLT)

- Website: plt.org
- Resources: Environmental education programs, lesson plans, and professional development for educators.

Earth Day Network

- Website: earthday.org
- Resources: Ideas for Earth Day activities, virtual events, and year-round environmental education initiatives.

These resources provide valuable information, tools, and support for schools looking to implement and enhance their sustainability practices. By leveraging these resources, schools can effectively address common sustainability challenges and make meaningful progress toward becoming more environmentally responsible.

Tools for Schools: Sustainability Calculators and Resources

This section outlines some valuable tools for schools.

Carbon Calculators

Cool School Challenge

- Website: coolschoolchallenge.org
- Description: A comprehensive program that helps schools measure and reduce their carbon footprint through student-led initiatives and carbon footprint calculators.

Carbon Footprint Calculator by Conservation International

- Website: conservation.org/carbon-footprint-calculator
- Description: A simple and intuitive tool for calculating the carbon footprint of individuals and institutions, including schools.

EPA Carbon Footprint Calculator

- Website: epa.gov/carbon-footprint-calculator
- Description: An easy-to-use calculator that helps schools estimate their

greenhouse gas emissions from various activities.

Cost Savings Calculators

ENERGY STAR Portfolio Manager

- Website: energystar.gov/portfoliomanager
- Description: A robust tool for tracking and managing energy and water consumption, allowing schools to calculate potential cost savings from energy efficiency improvements.

Building Upgrade Value Calculator by the U.S. Department of Energy

- Website: energy.gov/eere/buildings/building-upgrade-value-calculator
- Description: This tool helps schools estimate the financial returns and energy savings from various building upgrades.

Solar Savings Calculator by EnergySage

- Website: energysage.com/solar/calculator
- Description: A tool that allows schools to calculate potential savings from installing solar panels based on their location and energy usage.

Waste Reduction Tools

WasteWise Re-TRAC Connect by EPA

- Website: epa.gov/smm/wastewise
- Description: A tool that helps schools track waste reduction, recycling, and waste diversion activities to identify cost savings opportunities.

Zero Waste Audit Tool by Zero Waste International Alliance

- Website: zwia.org/zero-waste-definition
- Description: A comprehensive audit tool to help schools assess their waste production and identify ways to move towards zero waste.

Water Conservation Tools

WaterSense Water Budget Tool by EPA

- Website: epa.gov/watersense/water-budget-tool
- Description: A tool to help schools create a water budget and identify potential water savings through conservation measures.

Water Footprint Calculator by Water Footprint Network

- Website: waterfootprint.org
- Description: A calculator that allows schools to measure their water footprint and identify ways to reduce water use.

Sustainable Procurement Tools

Green Procurement Compilation by GSA

- Website: sftool.gov/greenprocurement
- Description: A tool to help schools identify environmentally preferable products and services to support sustainable procurement policies.

EPEAT Registry by Green Electronics Council

- Website: epeat.net
- Description: A registry of sustainable electronics, helping schools purchase environmentally friendly IT equipment.

Renewable Energy Tools

TOOLS FOR SCHOOLS: SUSTAINABILITY CALCULATORS AND RESOURCES

PVWatts Calculator by NREL

- Website: pvwatts.nrel.gov
- Description: A tool for estimating the energy production and cost savings of photovoltaic (PV) solar panels based on geographic location.

Wind Energy Potential Mapping by DOE

- Website: energy.gov/maps/wind-energy
- Description: A mapping tool to help schools assess the potential for wind energy installations on their property.

General Sustainability Tools

Sustainable Schools Project Toolkit by Shelburne Farms

- Website: sustainableschoolsproject.org
- Description: A toolkit offering resources, lesson plans, and assessment tools to help schools integrate sustainability into their curriculum and operations.

Green Classroom Professional Certificate by USGBC

- Website: usgbc.org/education/sessions/green-classroom-professional-certificate
- Description: A certification program that provides teachers with the knowledge to create healthy, sustainable learning environments.

These tools are designed to help schools measure, manage, and improve their sustainability practices, resulting in both environmental benefits and cost savings. By leveraging these resources, schools can make informed decisions and take actionable steps toward a more sustainable future.

Websites and Links

Here is an extended list of resources and useful websites for understanding the science of climate change:

Government and International Organizations

NASA Climate Change: Comprehensive data on climate change indicators, educational resources, and multimedia tools.

- NASA Climate Change

Environmental Protection Agency (EPA): Resources for educators and students, including climate indicators, science basics, and impacts.

- EPA Climate Change

National Oceanic and Atmospheric Administration (NOAA): Teaching materials, data sets, and multimedia resources for understanding climate science.

- NOAA Climate.gov

Intergovernmental Panel on Climate Change (IPCC): Assessment reports and scientific data on climate change.

WEBSITES AND LINKS

- IPCC

World Meteorological Organization (WMO): Climate updates and resources from the United Nations' specialized agency.

- WMO

Academic and Research Institutions

MIT Climate Portal: Educational resources, podcasts, and interactive tools for high school and college educators.

- MIT Climate Portal

Harvard University - Climate Change: Research and resources on climate science and policy.

- Harvard Climate Initiative

Yale Program on Climate Change Communication: Insights and data on public understanding and attitudes towards climate change.

- Yale Climate Communication

Non-Governmental Organizations

World Resources Institute (WRI): Detailed summaries of climate science and models projecting future climate changes.

- WRI

The Climate Reality Project: Information and campaigns on climate change, led by former Vice President Al Gore.

- The Climate Reality Project

Union of Concerned Scientists (UCS): Scientific analysis and advocacy on climate change and clean energy.

- UCS Climate Science

Educational and Informative Platforms

Khan Academy - Climate Change: Educational videos and articles explaining the basics of climate science.

- Khan Academy

National Geographic - Climate Change: Articles, infographics, and documentaries on climate science and impacts.

- National Geographic

BBC Climate Change: News, analysis, and scientific explanations about climate change.

- BBC Climate Change

The Guardian - Climate Crisis: In-depth reporting and analysis on global climate issues.

- The Guardian

Interactive and Data Visualization Tools

Climate Central: Interactive tools and maps that illustrate climate impacts and projections.

- Climate Central

Carbon Brief: Clear explanations, data visualizations, and maps on climate science and policy.

- Carbon Brief

Our World in Data - CO2 and Greenhouse Gas Emissions: Data and visualizations on global emissions and climate change.

- Our World in Data

Educational Games and Activities

Climate Kids (NASA): Interactive website for kids with activities, articles, and videos about climate change.

- Climate Kids

ENERGY STAR Kids: Educational games and tips on energy efficiency and climate change.

- ENERGY STAR Kids

These resources provide a comprehensive overview of climate science, educational tools, and actionable insights into addressing climate change.

Climate Change and Human Activity

Here are some key facts about the science of climate change and the role of human activities:

The Science of Climate Change

1. **Greenhouse Effect**: The greenhouse effect is a natural process where certain atmospheric gases trap heat, keeping the planet warm enough to support life. Human activities have increased concentrations of these greenhouse gases, enhancing the effect and leading to global warming (NASA Science) (NASA Science).
2. **Greenhouse Gases**: The main greenhouse gases are carbon dioxide (CO_2), methane (CH_4), nitrous oxide (N_2O), and fluorinated gases. CO_2 is the most significant due to its large volume and long atmospheric lifetime (US EPA) (MIT Climate Portal).
3. **Temperature Rise**: Since the late 19th century, the global average temperature has increased by approximately 1.2 degrees Celsius (2.2 degrees Fahrenheit), with most of this warming occurring in the last 35 years.
4. **Sea Level Rise**: Global sea levels have risen by about 8 inches (20 cm) over the past century, primarily due to the thermal expansion of seawater and the melting of glaciers and ice sheets.
5. **Extreme Weather Events**: Climate change is linked to increased frequency and severity of extreme weather events such as heatwaves,

hurricanes, droughts, and heavy rainfall. These events can significantly impact ecosystems, infrastructure, and human health.

Human Activities and Climate Change

1. **Fossil Fuel Combustion**: Burning fossil fuels for energy (coal, oil, and natural gas) is the largest source of CO_2 emissions, accounting for about 75% of global greenhouse gas emissions.
2. **Deforestation**: Cutting down forests reduces the planet's capacity to absorb CO_2, contributing to higher atmospheric CO_2 levels. Deforestation is responsible for about 10-15% of global emissions.
3. **Agriculture**: Agricultural practices release significant amounts of methane and nitrous oxide, potent greenhouse gases. Livestock digestion, rice paddies, and fertilizer use are major sources.
4. **Industrial Processes**: Certain industrial activities, such as cement production and the use of certain chemicals, emit CO_2 and other greenhouse gases.
5. **Waste Management**: Landfills produce methane as organic waste decomposes anaerobically. Improved waste management practices can reduce these emissions.

Mitigation and Adaptation

1. **Renewable Energy**: Transitioning to renewable energy sources like solar, wind, and hydroelectric power can significantly reduce greenhouse gas emissions.
2. **Energy Efficiency**: Improving energy efficiency in buildings, transportation, and industries can reduce energy demand and emissions.
3. **Afforestation and Reforestation**: Planting trees and restoring forests can increase carbon sequestration, helping to offset emissions.
4. **Sustainable Agriculture**: Adopting sustainable agricultural practices can reduce farming emissions and improve resilience to climate impacts.
5. **Climate Policies**: National and international policies like the Paris

Agreement aim to limit global warming and promote sustainable development.

These facts highlight the importance of understanding and addressing the human causes of climate change to mitigate its impacts and ensure a sustainable future.

References:

1. NASA Climate Change
2. EPA Climate Change
3. World Meteorological Organization
4. IPCC
5. National Geographic
6. Union of Concerned Scientists
7. Harvard Climate Change and Health
8. WHO Climate Change and Health

Key Facts: Human-made Climate Change

Here are 25 key facts about how human actions are contributing to climate change:

Greenhouse Gas Emissions

1. **Fossil Fuel Combustion**: Burning fossil fuels (coal, oil, and natural gas) for energy and transportation is the largest source of greenhouse gas emissions globally, releasing significant amounts of CO_2 into the atmosphere (NASA Science) (NASA Science).
2. **Deforestation**: Clearing forests for agriculture or urban development reduces the number of trees that can absorb CO_2, thus increasing atmospheric carbon levels (US EPA).
3. **Agriculture**: Agricultural activities, including livestock farming and rice paddies, release methane (CH_4), a potent greenhouse gas, and nitrous oxide (N_2O) through fertilization and manure management (MIT Climate Portal).
4. **Industrial Processes**: Industries such as cement production, chemical manufacturing, and metal smelting emit CO_2 and other greenhouse gases during their operations.

Transportation

1. **Vehicle Emissions**: Cars, trucks, airplanes, and ships burn fossil

fuels, emitting CO2 and other pollutants. Transportation is a major contributor to greenhouse gas emissions, accounting for about 14% globally.
2. **Aviation**: Air travel is particularly carbon-intensive, with the aviation industry contributing approximately 2.5% of global CO2 emissions.

Energy Production

1. **Coal-Fired Power Plants**: Coal-burning power plants are a significant source of CO2 emissions due to the high carbon content of coal.
2. **Natural Gas Production**: While cleaner than coal, natural gas production and use still result in CO2 and methane emissions, especially from leaks during extraction and transport.

Land Use and Urbanization

1. **Urban Heat Islands**: Urbanization leads to the creation of heat islands, where concrete and asphalt absorb and re-emit heat, increasing local temperatures and energy consumption for cooling.
2. **Soil Degradation**: Agricultural practices that degrade soil quality release stored carbon into the atmosphere, contributing to greenhouse gas emissions.

Waste Management

1. **Landfills**: Organic waste in landfills decomposes anaerobically, producing methane. Landfills are a significant source of methane emissions.
2. **Incineration**: Burning waste releases CO2 and other greenhouse gases, contributing to atmospheric pollution.

Industrial Agriculture

1. **Fertilizer Use**: Synthetic fertilizers release nitrous oxide, a greenhouse

gas that is 300 times more potent than CO2 over a 100-year period.
2. **Livestock Production**: Livestock, especially cattle, produce methane during digestion. Livestock farming is a significant source of methane emissions.

Energy Consumption

1. **Residential Energy Use**: Heating, cooling, and powering homes contribute to CO2 emissions, especially when the energy comes from fossil fuels.
2. **Appliance Use**: Household appliances and electronics, when used inefficiently, increase energy consumption and associated emissions.

Deforestation and Land Use

1. **Forest Fires**: Human activities that lead to forest fires release significant amounts of CO2 and reduce the number of trees available to absorb CO2.
2. **Peatland Destruction**: Draining and burning peatlands for agriculture and development releases stored carbon, contributing to greenhouse gas emissions.

Industrial Activities

1. **Cement Production**: Cement manufacturing is responsible for about 8% of global CO2 emissions due to the chemical processes involved in producing cement clinker.
2. **Chemical Industry**: The production of chemicals, including fertilizers and plastics, emits greenhouse gases during manufacturing and through the lifecycle of the products.

Consumer Habits

1. **Single-Use Plastics**: The production and disposal of single-use plastics contribute to greenhouse gas emissions and environmental pollution.
2. **Fast Fashion**: The fashion industry is a significant contributor to greenhouse gas emissions due to the energy-intensive processes involved in producing and transporting clothing.

Infrastructure Development

1. **Road Construction**: Building and maintaining roads involves the use of heavy machinery and materials that emit CO_2 during their production and use.
2. **Urban Sprawl**: Expanding urban areas lead to more vehicle use, higher energy consumption, and the destruction of natural habitats that can absorb CO_2.

Consumer Waste

1. **Electronic Waste**: The production, use, and disposal of electronic devices contribute to greenhouse gas emissions, particularly when e-waste is not properly managed.

These facts demonstrate the need for a comprehensive, collective effort to combat climate change, underscoring the importance of action across multiple sectors to mitigate these impacts.

Impacts of Climate Change on Human Health

Understanding the impact of climate change on human health is crucial for taking informed action. Here are some valuable resources and links to help individuals explore this topic in depth:

Government and International Organizations

Centers for Disease Control and Prevention (CDC) - Climate and Health: Provides information on how climate change affects health, including topics like extreme heat, air pollution, and vector-borne diseases.

- CDC - Climate and Health

World Health Organization (WHO) - Climate Change and Health: Offers a global perspective on the health impacts of climate change, including reports and action plans.

- WHO - Climate Change and Health

Environmental Protection Agency (EPA) - Climate Change and Human Health: Details the various ways climate change impacts health and provides resources for understanding and mitigating these effects.

- EPA - Climate Change and Human Health

Research and Academic Institutions

Harvard T.H. Chan School of Public Health - Climate Change and Health: Research and educational materials on how climate change affects human health, including articles, videos, and courses.

- Harvard Climate Change and Health

National Institutes of Health (NIH) - Climate Change and Human Health Literature Portal: A comprehensive database of scientific literature on the health impacts of climate change.

- NIH - Climate Change and Human Health Literature Portal

Non-Governmental Organizations

Climate Reality Project - Climate Change and Health: Information on the intersection of climate change and health, including personal stories and advocacy tips.

- Climate Reality Project - Health

Union of Concerned Scientists (UCS) - Climate Change and Your Health: Explains the science behind climate change's impact on health and provides resources for advocacy.

- UCS - Climate Change and Your Health

Educational and Informative Platforms

Khan Academy - Climate Change and Health: Educational videos and articles explaining the health impacts of climate change.

- Khan Academy - Climate Change and Health

National Geographic - Climate Change and Health: Articles and infographics detailing how climate change affects human health globally.

- National Geographic - Climate Change and Health

Reports and Publications

Lancet Countdown on Health and Climate Change: Annual reports tracking the impact of climate change on global health.

- Lancet Countdown

Global Health Alliance - Climate Change and Health: A collection of resources, research, and policy papers on the health impacts of climate change.

- Global Health Alliance

Action and Advocacy

Health Care Without Harm - Climate and Health: Resources for healthcare professionals and institutions on addressing climate change impacts on health.

- Health Care Without Harm

American Public Health Association (APHA) - Climate Change: Advocacy resources and information on the health impacts of climate change, aimed at public health professionals.

- APHA - Climate Change

Interactive Tools and Data Visualization

Climate Health and Equity Data Explorer by CDC: An interactive tool to explore the relationships between climate change, environmental hazards, and population health.

- CDC Climate Health and Equity Data Explorer

Climate Impact Lab - Climate and Health: Interactive maps and data visualizations showing the health impacts of climate change across the globe.

- Climate Impact Lab

These resources provide a comprehensive view of how climate change affects human health, offering tools, data, and actionable insights for individuals and communities.

Climate Actions in Schools

Here is a quick reference to some sustainable activities that schools can undertake to tackle climate change:

Energy Efficiency and Renewable Energy

Install Solar Panels: Schools can install solar panels to generate renewable energy, reduce electricity costs, and decrease their carbon footprint.

- EnergySage - Solar for Schools

Energy Audits and Upgrades: Conduct energy audits to identify areas for improvement and implement energy-efficient upgrades such as LED lighting, smart thermostats, and better insulation.

- EPA - Energy Efficiency for Schools

Sustainable Transportation

Promote Walking and Biking: Encourage students to walk or bike to school by providing bike racks and organizing "walk to school" days.

- Safe Routes to School

Carpool Programs: Establish carpool programs for students and staff to reduce the number of vehicles on the road.

- Carpool School Programs

Waste Reduction and Recycling

Comprehensive Recycling Programs: Implement recycling programs for paper, plastic, metal, and glass. Educate students on the importance of recycling and proper sorting.

- EPA - Recycling Basics

Composting: Set up a composting system for food waste from the cafeteria and organic waste from school grounds. Use the compost in school gardens.

- How to Compost at School

School Gardens and Green Spaces

School Gardens: Create and maintain school gardens where students can grow vegetables and learn about sustainable agriculture.

- KidsGardening - School Gardens

Tree Planting: Organize tree planting activities to increase green cover, enhance biodiversity, and educate students about the benefits of trees for the environment.

- Arbor Day Foundation - Tree Planting Programs

Curriculum and Education

Integrate Climate Education: Incorporate climate change education into the curriculum to teach students about the science of climate change, its impacts, and mitigation strategies.

- Climate Literacy and Energy Awareness Network

Environmental Clubs: Establish environmental clubs where students can participate in sustainability projects, learn about environmental issues, and advocate for green practices.

- Eco-Schools USA

Sustainable Practices and Initiatives

Green Building Practices: When renovating or building new facilities, use sustainable materials and green building practices to minimize the environmental impact.

- US Green Building Council - LEED for Schools

Water Conservation: Install water-saving fixtures, fix leaks promptly, and educate students on the importance of water conservation.

- EPA - WaterSense for Schools

Community Engagement

Green Fundraisers: Organize fundraisers that promote sustainability, such as selling reusable water bottles or hosting e-waste recycling events.

- Green Fundraising Ideas

Collaborate with Local Environmental Organizations: Partner with local environmental organizations to participate in community clean-ups, conservation projects, and educational workshops.

- Local Environmental Partnerships

Zero Waste Initiatives

Reduce Single-Use Plastics: Eliminate single-use plastics in the cafeteria and encourage students to use reusable containers and utensils.

- Zero Waste Schools

By engaging in these activities, schools can reduce their own carbon footprint and educate and inspire the next generation to take action against climate change.

Here are some sustainable activities that schools can undertake to tackle climate change:

Energy Efficiency and Renewable Energy

Install Solar Panels: Schools can install solar panels to generate renewable energy, reduce electricity costs, and decrease their carbon footprint.

- EnergySage - Solar for Schools

Energy Audits and Upgrades: Conduct energy audits to identify areas for improvement and implement energy-efficient upgrades such as LED lighting, smart thermostats, and better insulation.

- EPA - Energy Efficiency for Schools

Sustainable Transportation

Promote Walking and Biking: Encourage students to walk or bike to school by providing bike racks and organizing "walk to school" days.

- Safe Routes to School

Carpool Programs: Establish carpool programs for students and staff to reduce the number of vehicles on the road.

- Carpool School Programs

Waste Reduction and Recycling

Comprehensive Recycling Programs: Implement recycling programs for paper, plastic, metal, and glass. Educate students on the importance of recycling and proper sorting.

- EPA - Recycling Basics

Composting: Set up a composting system for food waste from the cafeteria and organic waste from school grounds. Use the compost in school gardens.

- How to Compost at School

School Gardens and Green Spaces

School Gardens: Create and maintain school gardens where students can grow vegetables and learn about sustainable agriculture.

- KidsGardening - School Gardens

Tree Planting: Organize tree planting activities to increase green cover, enhance biodiversity, and educate students about the benefits of trees for the environment.

- Arbor Day Foundation - Tree Planting Programs

Curriculum and Education

Integrate Climate Education: Incorporate climate change education into the curriculum to teach students about the science of climate change, its impacts, and mitigation strategies.

- Climate Literacy and Energy Awareness Network

Environmental Clubs: Establish environmental clubs where students can participate in sustainability projects, learn about environmental issues, and advocate for green practices.

- Eco-Schools USA

Sustainable Practices and Initiatives

Green Building Practices: When renovating or building new facilities, use sustainable materials and green building practices to minimize the environmental impact.

- US Green Building Council - LEED for Schools

Water Conservation: Install water-saving fixtures, fix leaks promptly, and educate students on the importance of water conservation.

- EPA - WaterSense for Schools

Community Engagement

Green Fundraisers: Organize fundraisers that promote sustainability, such as selling reusable water bottles or hosting e-waste recycling events.

- Green Fundraising Ideas

Collaborate with Local Environmental Organizations: Partner with local environmental organizations to participate in community clean-ups, conservation projects, and educational workshops.

- Local Environmental Partnerships

Zero Waste Initiatives

Reduce Single-Use Plastics: Eliminate single-use plastics in the cafeteria and encourage students to use reusable containers and utensils.

- Zero Waste Schools

By engaging in these activities, schools can not only reduce their own carbon footprint but also educate and inspire the next generation to take action against climate change.

Individual Climate Action

Here are some key facts about how individual actions can help address climate change:

Energy Conservation and Efficiency

1. **Reducing Energy Use**: Simple actions like turning off lights when not in use, using energy-efficient appliances, and insulating homes can significantly reduce energy consumption and carbon footprints. Energy-efficient homes use 20-30% less energy than standard homes.
2. **Switching to Renewable Energy**: Individuals can reduce their carbon footprint by choosing renewable energy sources, such as solar or wind power, for their homes. This can cut household carbon emissions by as much as 50-80%.

Transportation Choices

1. **Using Public Transportation**: Opting for public transport, biking, or walking instead of driving can significantly reduce greenhouse gas emissions. Public transportation produces 76% fewer emissions per passenger mile compared to single-occupancy vehicles (NASA Science).
2. **Driving Efficiently**: When driving is necessary, maintaining a fuel-efficient vehicle and practicing eco-driving techniques, such as avoiding rapid acceleration and maintaining steady speeds, can improve fuel

economy by up to 40% (NASA Science) (US EPA).

Sustainable Diets and Food Choices

1. **Reducing Meat Consumption**: The production of meat, especially beef, is a major contributor to greenhouse gas emissions. Reducing meat consumption and opting for plant-based diets can lower individual carbon footprints. A vegetarian diet can reduce food-related emissions by about 50% (MIT Climate Portal) .
2. **Minimizing Food Waste**: About one-third of all food produced is wasted, contributing to unnecessary emissions. Planning meals, storing food properly, and composting organic waste can reduce this impact .

Waste Reduction and Recycling

1. **Reducing, Reusing, and Recycling**: Proper waste management practices, such as reducing single-use plastics, reusing items, and recycling, can decrease the amount of waste that ends up in landfills and reduce greenhouse gas emissions associated with waste processing .
2. **Composting**: Composting organic waste reduces methane emissions from landfills and produces valuable compost that can improve soil health and carbon sequestration .

Water Conservation

1. **Saving Water**: Using water efficiently, such as taking shorter showers, fixing leaks, and using water-saving fixtures, can reduce energy consumption for water heating and distribution, thereby lowering greenhouse gas emissions .

Supporting Climate-Friendly Policies and Practices

1. **Advocating for Climate Action**: Individuals can support policies that promote renewable energy, energy efficiency, and sustainable practices by voting for leaders who prioritize climate action and participating in advocacy efforts.
2. **Educating and Raising Awareness**: Educating others about climate change and its impacts can inspire collective action. Participating in community initiatives and supporting environmental organizations can amplify individual efforts.

References:

1. EPA - Energy Efficiency
2. Energy.gov - Energy Saving Tips
3. NRDC - Renewable Energy
4. Green America - Solar Power
5. American Public Transportation Association
6. Union of Concerned Scientists - Transportation
7. EPA - Smart Driving
8. FuelEconomy.gov - Driving Tips
9. Harvard T.H. Chan School of Public Health - Diet and Climate Change
10. World Resources Institute - Shifting Diets
11. FAO - Food Loss and Waste
12. EPA - Food Recovery
13. EPA - Reducing and Reusing
14. NRDC - Recycling
15. Compost Foundation - Composting Benefits
16. EPA - Composting at Home
17. WaterSense - Water Saving Tips
18. Energy.gov - Water Heating
19. Climate Reality Project - Take Action
20. Citizens' Climate Lobby
21. EarthDay.org - Climate Action
22. 350.org – Campaigns

100 Individual Climate Actions

Here is a list of 100 actions individuals can take to tackle climate change, along with explanations and references:

1. **Reduce, Reuse, Recycle** - Minimizing waste conserves resources and reduces greenhouse gas emissions (EPA).
2. **Use Energy-Efficient Appliances** - Energy Star appliances use less energy and save money (Energy Star).
3. **Install Solar Panels** - Solar energy reduces reliance on fossil fuels (SEIA).
4. **Use LED Lighting** - LEDs use less energy and last longer (Department of Energy).
5. **Unplug Devices When Not in Use** - Reduces "phantom" energy use (NRDC).
6. **Insulate Your Home** - Improves energy efficiency and reduces heating/cooling needs (EPA).
7. **Use a Programmable Thermostat** - Optimizes heating and cooling, reducing energy use (Energy Star).
8. **Choose Renewable Energy** - Switch to a green energy provider (Green Power Partnership).
9. **Drive Less** - Walking, biking, or using public transport reduces carbon emissions (EPA).
10. **Carpool or Use Ride-Sharing** - Reduces the number of

vehicles on the road (NRDC).
11. **Maintain Your Vehicle** - Regular maintenance improves fuel efficiency (Department of Energy).
12. **Switch to an Electric or Hybrid Car** - Reduces reliance on fossil fuels (Union of Concerned Scientists).
13. **Use Public Transportation** - Lessens individual carbon footprint (American Public Transportation Association).
14. **Fly Less** - Air travel has a high carbon footprint (EPA).
15. **Purchase Carbon Offsets for Flights** - Helps balance out emissions (Carbonfund.org).
16. **Support Carbon Pricing Policies** - Economic incentives to reduce emissions (World Bank).
17. **Eat Less Meat** - Livestock farming is a major source of greenhouse gases (UN FAO).
18. **Adopt a Plant-Based Diet** - Reduces carbon footprint significantly (Environmental Research Letters).
19. **Buy Locally Sourced Food** - Reduces transportation emissions (NRDC).
20. **Grow Your Own Food** - Minimizes food miles and promotes sustainable practices (EPA).
21. **Compost Organic Waste** - Reduces landfill waste and produces natural fertilizer (EPA).
22. **Avoid Single-Use Plastics** - Reduces pollution and fossil fuel use (Plastic Pollution Coalition).
23. **Support Sustainable Fashion** - Reduces environmental impact of clothing production (Good On You).
24. **Buy Second-Hand Clothing** - Decreases demand for new clothing (EPA).
25. **Donate Unwanted Items** - Extends product life and reduces waste (EPA).
26. **Reduce Water Use** - Conserves energy used in water treatment and heating (EPA).
27. **Fix Leaks Promptly** - Saves water and reduces energy costs

(EPA).

28. **Install Low-Flow Fixtures** - Reduces water use and energy needed to heat water (EPA).
29. **Use Cold Water for Laundry** - Saves energy used for heating water (Department of Energy).
30. **Air Dry Clothes** - Reduces energy use from dryers (NRDC).
31. **Choose Sustainable Cleaning Products** - Reduces chemical pollution (EPA).
32. **Reduce Paper Use** - Saves trees and reduces carbon footprint (NRDC).
33. **Use E-Tickets and E-Bills** - Reduces paper waste (EPA).
34. **Plant Trees** - Absorbs CO2 and provides oxygen (Arbor Day Foundation).
35. **Support Reforestation Projects** - Helps restore ecosystems (One Tree Planted).
36. **Use a Rain Barrel** - Collects rainwater for garden use (EPA).
37. **Install a Green Roof** - Improves insulation and reduces urban heat island effect (EPA).
38. **Participate in Community Cleanups** - Reduces pollution and fosters community spirit (Keep America Beautiful).
39. **Educate Yourself on Climate Issues** - Informed individuals can make better choices (IPCC).
40. **Advocate for Climate Policies** - Supports systemic change (Citizens' Climate Lobby).
41. **Vote for Climate-Conscious Candidates** - Influences policy at all levels (League of Conservation Voters).
42. **Join Environmental Groups** - Collective action amplifies impact (Sierra Club).
43. **Support Renewable Energy Projects** - Drives market demand for clean energy (SEIA).
44. **Reduce Air Conditioning Use** - Saves energy and reduces emissions (NRDC).
45. **Use Sustainable Transportation** - Biking or walking for

short trips (EPA).
46. **Invest in Green Technologies** - Supports innovation and growth in sustainable industries (Clean Technica).
47. **Support Local Farmers** - Reduces transportation emissions and supports local economies (Farmers Market Coalition).
48. **Participate in Meatless Mondays** - Reduces meat consumption (Meatless Monday).
49. **Use Reusable Shopping Bags** - Reduces plastic waste (NRDC).
50. **Pack Waste-Free Lunches** - Minimizes packaging waste (EPA).
51. **Purchase Energy-Efficient Windows** - Improves home insulation (Department of Energy).
52. **Install a Smart Meter** - Monitors and reduces energy use (Energy Star).
53. **Use Eco-Friendly Pest Control** - Reduces chemical use (EPA).
54. **Choose a Fuel-Efficient Car** - Reduces emissions and saves on fuel costs (EPA).
55. **Support Fair Trade Products** - Encourages sustainable farming practices (Fair Trade USA).
56. **Reduce Food Waste** - Saves resources and reduces methane emissions from landfills (NRDC).
57. **Learn to Repair Items** - Extends product life and reduces waste (iFixit).
58. **Use Recycled Products** - Supports recycling industry and reduces waste (EPA).
59. **Choose Minimal Packaging** - Reduces waste and pollution (NRDC).
60. **Support Sustainable Tourism** - Minimizes environmental impact (Sustainable Travel International).
61. **Volunteer for Environmental Projects** - Directly contributes to conservation efforts (Conservation Volunteers

International).

62. **Support Wildlife Conservation** - Protects biodiversity and ecosystems (WWF).
63. **Avoid Palm Oil Products** - Reduces deforestation and habitat destruction (Rainforest Action Network).
64. **Practice Sustainable Fishing** - Protects marine ecosystems (Monterey Bay Aquarium Seafood Watch).
65. **Use a Bike for Short Trips** - Reduces emissions and improves health (EPA).
66. **Join a Car-Share Program** - Reduces the number of cars on the road (Zipcar).
67. **Use Public Libraries** - Reduces the need for new books and resources (ALA).
68. **Buy Long-Lasting Products** - Reduces waste and resource use (NRDC).
69. **Use Natural Light** - Reduces the need for artificial lighting (Department of Energy).
70. **Reduce Heating and Cooling Use** - Saves energy and reduces emissions (NRDC).
71. **Support Organic Farming** - Reduces chemical use and promotes soil health (Rodale Institute).
72. **Use Electric Lawn Equipment** - Reduces emissions compared to gasoline-powered equipment (EPA).
73. **Choose Low-Emission Shipping Options** - Reduces transportation emissions (EPA).
74. **Support Marine Conservation** - Protects ocean ecosystems (Ocean Conservancy).
75. **Use Public Parks and Natural Spaces** - Encourages preservation of green spaces (NRPA).
76. **Conserve Forests** - Protects carbon sinks and biodiversity (WWF).
77. **Participate in Local Climate Actions** - Engages community and raises awareness (350.org).

78. **Support Sustainable Building Practices** - Promotes energy-efficient construction (USGBC).
79. **Invest in Green Bonds** - Supports environmental projects (Climate Bonds Initiative).
80. **Use Biodegradable Products** - Reduces waste and pollution (EPA).
81. **Choose Certified Sustainable Products** - Ensures responsible production (FSC, MSC).
82. **Install a Tankless Water Heater** - Improves energy efficiency (Department of Energy).
83. **Avoid Products with Microbeads** - Reduces plastic pollution (EPA).
84. **Use a Water Filter** - Reduces bottled water consumption (EPA).
85. **Support Indigenous Land Rights** - Protects ecosystems and biodiversity (Amazon Watch).
86. **Choose Low VOC Products** - Reduces indoor air pollution (EPA).
87. **Use Cloth Diapers** - Reduces waste compared to disposables (NRDC).
88. **Buy Fair Trade Coffee and Chocolate** - Supports sustainable farming practices (Fair Trade USA).
89. **Support Clean Water Initiatives** - Protects water resources (Water.org).
90. **Participate in Energy Audits** - Identifies ways to improve home energy efficiency (Energy Star).
91. **Practice Permaculture** - Promotes sustainable agriculture (Permaculture Institute).
92. **Use a Bike Trailer for Errands** - Reduces car use (EPA).
93. **Support Eco-Friendly Legislation** - Encourages systemic change (NRDC).
94. **Use Natural Fertilizers** - Reduces chemical pollution (EPA).
95. **Practice Responsible Pet Ownership** - Reduces environ-

mental impact (ASPCA).
96. **Choose Sustainable Building Materials** - Reduces environmental footprint (USGBC).
97. **Use Renewable Energy Certificates** - Supports renewable energy projects (Green Power Partnership).
98. **Support Urban Farming** - Promotes local food production (Urban Farm).
99. **Choose Plant-Based Cleaning Products** - Reduces chemical use (EPA).
100. **Engage in Climate Conversations** - Raises awareness and promotes action (Climate Reality Project).

References:

- EPA (Environmental Protection Agency). Energy Star
- NRDC (Natural Resources Defense Council). NRDC
- SEIA (Solar Energy Industries Association). SEIA
- Union of Concerned Scientists. UCS
- UN FAO (Food and Agriculture Organization). FAO
- IPCC (Intergovernmental Panel on Climate Change). IPCC
- WWF (World Wildlife Fund). WWF
- Ocean Conservancy. Ocean Conservancy
- USGBC (U.S. Green Building Council). USGBC
- Climate Reality Project. Climate Reality

Resources for Individual Climate Action

Here is a curated list of resources and websites to help individuals take meaningful climate action:

General Climate Action

Climate Reality Project: Provides information on how to take action on climate change, including personal steps and community initiatives.

- Climate Reality Project - Take Action

EPA - What You Can Do About Climate Change: Strategies for individuals to reduce their carbon footprint, including energy conservation, transportation choices, and waste reduction.

- EPA - What You Can Do

United Nations - ActNow: The UN's campaign for individual action on climate change and sustainability. Includes tips on saving energy, reducing waste, and advocating for change.

- UN ActNow

Sustainable Living

EarthDay.org - Climate Action Toolkit: Offers a toolkit for individuals, including tips on sustainable living, reducing carbon footprints, and advocating for policy change.

- EarthDay.org Toolkit

WWF - Sustainable Living: Tips and guides on how to live more sustainably, covering topics such as energy use, food choices, and transportation.

- WWF Sustainable Living

National Resources Defense Council (NRDC) - Live Green: Practical tips for living more sustainably, including energy-saving ideas, green shopping, and reducing waste.

- NRDC Live Green

Energy Conservation

ENERGY STAR: Offers tips on how to save energy at home and in the workplace, including energy-efficient appliances and home improvements.

- ENERGY STAR

Department of Energy - Energy Saver: Comprehensive guide on energy-saving techniques and technologies for homes and businesses.

- DOE Energy Saver

Transportation

Bike League - Bicycle Friendly America: Information on how to make cycling a part of daily life, including tips on commuting and advocating for bike-friendly communities.

- Bike League

Smart Growth America - Transportation Choices: Resources on advocating for better public transportation and creating walkable, bikeable communities.

- Smart Growth America

Food and Agriculture

Sustainable Table: Information on how food choices impact the environment and tips for sustainable eating.

- Sustainable Table

FoodPrint: Offers resources on reducing food waste, sustainable diets, and the environmental impact of food production.

- FoodPrint

Waste Reduction

Zero Waste Home: Tips and resources on how to live a zero-waste lifestyle, including reducing plastic use and composting.

- Zero Waste Home

Plastic Pollution Coalition: Information and resources on reducing plastic use and advocating for plastic-free alternatives.

- Plastic Pollution Coalition

RESOURCES FOR INDIVIDUAL CLIMATE ACTION

Advocacy and Community Action

Citizens' Climate Lobby: Resources for advocating for climate policy, including how to engage with local governments and policymakers.

- Citizens' Climate Lobby

350.org: Global grassroots movement to solve the climate crisis, with resources on organizing and participating in climate actions.

- 350.org

Sierra Club - Climate and Energy: Guides on how to get involved in climate advocacy and campaigns for clean energy.

- Sierra Club

Education and Awareness

Climate Action Network: A global network of organizations promoting government and individual action on climate change.

- Climate Action Network

TED Countdown: A global initiative to champion and accelerate solutions to the climate crisis, including talks, articles, and action guides.

- TED Countdown

These resources offer a range of actions you can take, from personal lifestyle changes to community and policy advocacy, helping you contribute effectively to climate action.

Carbon Footprint Reduction at Home

Households can take several actions to reduce their carbon footprint. Here are some key strategies:

Energy Efficiency

1. **Use Energy-Efficient Appliances**: Replacing old appliances with EN-ERGY STAR-rated ones can reduce energy consumption significantly. For example, an ENERGY STAR refrigerator uses 15% less energy than a non-certified model (NASA Science) (NASA Science).
2. **Insulate Your Home**: Proper insulation in walls, attics, and floors can reduce heating and cooling costs by up to 20% (US EPA) (MIT Climate Portal).
3. **LED Lighting**: Switching to LED bulbs can save about 75% of energy compared to incandescent bulbs and last 25 times longer.

Renewable Energy

1. **Install Solar Panels**: Solar panels can drastically reduce your electricity bills and carbon footprint. A typical residential solar panel system can offset 3-4 tons of CO2 annually.
2. **Choose Green Energy Plans**: Many utilities offer green energy options that source electricity from renewable energy. Switching to such plans can support the growth of renewable energy and reduce your

household's carbon emissions.

Water Conservation

1. **Low-Flow Fixtures**: Installing low-flow showerheads and faucets can reduce water use and the energy needed to heat water, cutting emissions and saving money.
2. **Fix Leaks**: A leaky faucet can waste up to 3,000 gallons of water per year. Fixing leaks reduces water waste and the energy required for water heating.

Transportation

1. **Reduce Car Use**: Walking, biking, carpooling, or using public transport can significantly reduce your household's carbon emissions. Reducing car use by 20 miles per week can cut emissions by about 1,000 pounds of CO_2 annually.
2. **Electric Vehicles**: Switching to an electric vehicle (EV) can reduce your transportation emissions. EVs emit fewer greenhouse gases and air pollutants over their lifetime compared to traditional gasoline cars.

Sustainable Food Choices

1. **Eat Less Meat**: Reducing meat consumption, especially beef, can lower your carbon footprint. A plant-based diet can reduce food-related greenhouse gas emissions by up to 50%.
2. **Local and Seasonal Foods**: Eating locally grown and seasonal foods reduces emissions from transportation and storage.

Waste Reduction

1. **Recycle and Compost**: Recycling and composting can significantly reduce the amount of waste sent to landfills, which emit methane, a

potent greenhouse gas. Composting organic waste reduces methane emissions and produces valuable compost for gardening.
2. **Reduce Single-Use Plastics**: Using reusable bags, bottles, and containers can reduce plastic waste and its associated carbon footprint.

Household Practices

1. **Smart Thermostats**: A smart thermostat can optimize heating and cooling, saving energy and reducing emissions. It can save households up to 10-12% on heating and 15% on cooling costs.
2. **Laundry Practices**: Washing clothes in cold water and air-drying them can save energy. Washing in cold water can save up to 90% of the energy a washing machine uses.

References:

1. ENERGY STAR - Appliances
2. Energy.gov - Insulation
3. Energy.gov - Lighting
4. Solar Energy Industries Association
5. Green Energy Plans
6. EPA - WaterSense
7. Water Conservation Tips
8. Public Transportation Benefits
9. Union of Concerned Scientists - EVs
10. Harvard T.H. Chan School of Public Health - Diet and Climate Change
11. World Resources Institute - Shifting Diets
12. Local Foods - EPA
13. Zero Waste Home
14. EPA - Composting
15. Smart Thermostats
16. Cold Water Washing

Useful Tools and Resources for Homes

Here are some valuable resources, including carbon calculators and websites that offer tips and tools for supporting a sustainable lifestyle and creating a climate-friendly home:

Carbon Calculators

EPA Carbon Footprint Calculator: This tool helps you estimate your household's carbon footprint and find ways to reduce it.

- EPA Carbon Footprint Calculator

Carbon Footprint Calculator by Conservation International: This tool provides a detailed breakdown of your carbon footprint and offers tips for reduction.

- Conservation International Carbon Calculator

CoolClimate Network Carbon Calculator: Developed by UC Berkeley, this calculator helps you understand your carbon footprint and offers personalized action plans.

- CoolClimate Network Calculator

WWF Footprint Calculator: Measures your ecological footprint and suggests ways to reduce your environmental impact.

- WWF Footprint Calculator

Sustainable Living Resources

Sustainable Living Guide by WWF: Offers practical advice on how to live more sustainably, including energy-saving tips, reducing waste, and making sustainable food choices.

- WWF Sustainable Living

EarthDay.org Sustainable Living Tips: Provides a range of tips for sustainable living, covering topics such as waste reduction, energy conservation, and sustainable transportation.

- EarthDay.org Tips

Sustainable Lifestyle Resource Hub by National Geographic: Articles and guides on how to make sustainable choices in various aspects of daily life.

- National Geographic Sustainable Lifestyle

Climate-Friendly Home Resources

Energy Saver Guide by the U.S. Department of Energy: Comprehensive guide to energy efficiency for your home, including tips on heating, cooling, appliances, and lighting.

- DOE Energy Saver Guide

ENERGY STAR Home Improvement: Offers tips and tools for making

- ENERGY STAR Home Improvement

Home Energy Audit by the U.S. Department of Energy: Step-by-step guide to conducting a home energy audit to identify areas for energy-saving improvements.

- DOE Home Energy Audit

Waste Reduction and Recycling

Zero Waste Home: Provides resources and tips for reducing waste and living a zero-waste lifestyle.

- Zero Waste Home

EPA Reduce, Reuse, Recycle: Information and tips on how to reduce waste and recycle effectively.

- EPA Reduce, Reuse, Recycle

Sustainable Transportation

Bike League - Bike Friendly Communities: Information on how to support and participate in bike-friendly initiatives and communities.

- Bike League

Alternative Fuels Data Center by the U.S. Department of Energy: Resources on alternative fuels and advanced vehicle technologies to reduce transportation emissions.

- Alternative Fuels Data Center

Sustainable Food Choices

EAT-Lancet Commission on Food, Planet, Health: Guidelines and resources for sustainable diets that promote human health and environmental sustainability.

- EAT-Lancet

Sustainable Table: Information on the impact of food choices on the environment and tips for eating sustainably.

- Sustainable Table

By utilizing these resources, you can take actionable steps to reduce your carbon footprint and adopt a more sustainable lifestyle.

Community-led Climate Action

Here is a list of activities that people can do in their communities to tackle climate change:

Community Gardening and Urban Agriculture

Start a Community Garden: Create a shared space where community members can grow their own fruits and vegetables. This promotes local food production and reduces the carbon footprint associated with transporting food.

- American Community Gardening Association

Promote Urban Agriculture: Encourage urban farming initiatives, such as rooftop gardens and vertical farming, to increase local food production and green urban spaces.

- Urban Agriculture: Best Practices and Possibilities

Renewable Energy and Energy Efficiency

Organize a Solar Group Buy: Communities can come together to purchase solar panels in bulk, reducing costs and increasing the adoption of renewable energy.

- Solarize Campaigns

Energy Audits and Efficiency Upgrades: Promote community-wide energy audits and encourage residents to implement energy-efficient upgrades such as LED lighting, better insulation, and smart thermostats.

- Home Energy Audits

Sustainable Transportation

Carpooling and Ride-Sharing Programs: Establish local carpooling or ride-sharing programs to reduce the number of vehicles on the road, lowering emissions.

- Carpool World

Bike Sharing and Safe Cycling Infrastructure: Implement bike-sharing programs and advocate for better cycling infrastructure to promote biking as a sustainable mode of transportation.

- Bike Share Programs

Waste Reduction and Recycling

Zero Waste Initiatives: Start zero waste programs that encourage residents to reduce, reuse, and recycle. Hold workshops on composting and waste reduction techniques.

- Zero Waste Home

Community Recycling Drives: Organize recycling drives to collect items that are not typically picked up by regular recycling services, such as electronics and hazardous materials.

- How to Plan a Community Recycling Event

Education and Advocacy

Host Climate Education Workshops: Offer workshops and seminars to educate community members about climate change, its impacts, and what they can do to help.

- Climate Reality Project

Advocate for Climate-Friendly Policies: Mobilize the community to support local, state, and national policies that promote renewable energy, energy efficiency, and sustainable practices.

- Citizens' Climate Lobby

Green Spaces and Conservation

Tree Planting Programs: Organize tree planting events to increase urban tree cover, which helps sequester carbon, reduce heat islands, and improve air quality.

- Arbor Day Foundation

Conserve Local Ecosystems: Engage in activities that protect and restore local ecosystems, such as wetlands, forests, and watersheds.

- The Nature Conservancy

Sustainable Living Practices

Tool Libraries and Repair Cafés: Create community tool libraries where residents can borrow tools, and establish repair cafés where people can learn to fix household items instead of discarding them.

- Tool Libraries
- Repair Café

Support Local and Sustainable Businesses: Encourage the community to buy from local, sustainable businesses and farmers' markets to reduce the carbon footprint associated with goods transportation.

- Local Harvest

These activities help reduce the community's carbon footprint and foster a sense of community and collective environmental responsibility.

If you found this book helpful, we would appreciate it if you left us a favorable review!

*To receive periodic updates and **free promos** of our books and research, please sign up for our newsletters at ashpachauri.com/contact or scan the QR code below to register.*

COMMUNITY-LED CLIMATE ACTION

About the Author

Dr. Ash Pachauri, PhD

Dr. Ash Pachauri has a PhD in behavioral science and technology and a master's in international management. Having worked with McKinsey & Company before pursuing a career in the social development arena, Dr. Pachauri's experience in public health and sustainable development emerges from a range of initiatives. Notably, he has made significant contributions to the Bill & Melinda Gates Foundation by contributing to its public health and community agenda, the UN by focusing on youth, health, and the Sustainable Development Goals (SDGs), and the Center for Disease Control program interventions in the US by focusing on community interventions, especially for vulnerable youth. He has also been instrumental in founding and building the POP Movement and the World Sustainable Development Forum. He is a technical adviser to the World Health Organization on Self-Care global guidelines to support youth, communities, and global governments.

Dr. Pachauri has been a pioneer in the use of information technology for development. His innovative approaches have been key to spearheading community—and youth-led self-care interventions, leading to global capacity building and adoption of self-care among youth. As a master trainer in behavior change communications and strategic leadership, Dr. Pachauri has led over 20,000 workshops, events, and global outreach to youth and communities to promote global health and climate action.

Widely published, winner of the prestigious Overseas Research Scholarship, awarded for advanced studies in the U.K., and recognized for his academic achievements, Dr. Pachauri's awards and recognitions reflect his significant contributions to the field. The United Nations has recognized Dr. Pachauri for his dedication and leadership in their flagship publication, "Portraits of Commitment," A testament to his influence in the field. In 2021, he was awarded the GlobalMindED Inclusive Leadership Award for action in Energy and Sustainability, a recognition of his commitment to inclusive and sustainable development among young people worldwide. He is an Associate Fellow of the World Academy of Art and Science, a position that underscores his academic standing. Dr. Pachauri serves on the Boards and Advisory groups of several organizations and initiatives worldwide, including the global movement on bone health, the Climate Change Coalition, and the Global Union of Scientists for Peace. He demonstrates leadership and influence in the global health and climate action community.

Dr. Saroj Pachauri, MD, PhD, DPH

Dr. Saroj Pachauri, a dedicated public health physician, has made a significant impact through her extensive research on gender, youth, family planning, maternal and child health, sexual and reproductive health and rights, and HIV and AIDS. Her contributions are academic and practical, as she established the South and East Asia Population Council's regional office in India, a testament to her commitment to improving public health. Her exceptional work was recognized in 2011 when she was awarded the prestigious title of Distinguished Scholar, a rare honor that speaks volumes about her contributions to the field.

She worked with the Ford Foundation's New Delhi Office (1983-1994) and supported child survival, women's health, sexual and reproductive health, and HIV and AIDS programs. Before that, she worked with the International Fertility Research Program (IFRP), which was later renamed Family Health International (1971-1975), and the India Fertility Research Program (1975-1983). She designed and monitored multi-centric clinical trials globally to assess the safety and effectiveness of fertility control technologies. From 1962 to 1971, as faculty of the Departments of Preventive and Social Medicine at the Lady Hardinge Medical College, New Delhi, and the Institute of Medicine Sciences, Varanasi, she helped to develop this new discipline.

She has published eleven books and contributed chapters to 20 books. Her books cover a wide range of topics, including self-care, women's health, and youth, which have been instrumental in shaping the discourse in the field of public health. She has over 100 publications in peer-reviewed journals and several articles in print media.

www.ingramcontent.com/pod-product-compliance
Lightning Source LLC
Chambersburg PA
CBHW071918210526
45479CB00002B/472